Receiving God's Promises through Adversity

ALS – Memoir of a Caregiver

A Journey Through Fire

Shirley A. Knight

(ALS – Memoir of a Caregiver)

Copyright© 2011 by Shirley. A. Knight

New edition 2015

All rights reserved. Except as permitted under the U.S. Copyright Act of 1976, no Part of the publication may be reproduced, distributed, or transmitted in any form or by any means, or stored in a database or retrieval system without the prior written permission of the author.

Bible scripture quotations, unless otherwise indicated, are taken from the New King James Version. Copyright © 1982 by Thomas Nelson, Inc. Used by permission. All rights reserved.

Shirley-knight@comcast.net

Powell, Tennessee

http://www.AJourneyThroughFire.blogspot.com

Printed in the United States of America

A Journey Through Fire: ALS - Memoir of a Caregiver/ Shirley A. Knight — 1st edition

When you pass through the waters,
I will be with you;
And through the rivers, they shall
not overflow you.
When you walk through the fire,
you shall not be burned,
nor shall the flames scorch you.

For I am the Lord your God,
The Holy One of Israel, your Savior....

Isaiah 43:2-3

For Bill

You left your footprints on my heart.

Contents

Dedication   vii
Acknowledgements   xi
Introduction   xiii

Chapter 1:	A Pink Marble Stone	1
Chapter 2:	The Journey Begins	9
Chapter 3:	Waiting and Praying	19
Chapter 4:	A Dreadful Diagnosis	27
Chapter 5:	The Mystery Affliction	35
Chapter 6:	Is God Watching?	43
Chapter 7:	Searching for Hope	53
Chapter 8:	Fear Filled Nights	61
Chapter 9:	Going Home	69
Chapter 10:	A Clinical Trial	77
Chapter 11:	Longing for a Miracle	85
Chapter 12:	All Things for Good	93
Chapter 13:	A Wish Fulfilled	101

Chapter 14:	Loss and Helplessness	111
Chapter 15:	Frustration and Fear	121
Chapter 16:	Added Burdens	133
Chapter 17:	Cancer Care	141
Chapter 18:	God is Still at Work	149
Chapter 19:	Acceptance	157
Chapter 20:	Sustaining Grace	165
Chapter 21:	Difficult Decisions	175
Chapter 22:	The Everlasting Arms	185
Chapter 23:	What God Allows	193
Chapter 24:	A Caregiver's Anguish	203
Chapter 25:	Deepening Distress	213
Chapter 26:	A Turning Point	221
Chapter 27:	Letting Go	229
Chapter 28:	It won't be Long	237
Chapter 29:	He Himself is Our Peace	245
Chapter 30:	Memories	253
Epilogue		261
End Notes		267
Helpful Websites		271

Acknowledgements

A very special thank you to:

Our sons, Bill Jr., and John...you were always there when I needed you. He loved you both beyond words. Our grandsons, Justin, John Morgan, Sean, and Andrew...you were our light in the darkness. Our little granddaughter, Emma Grace...Papaw never got to meet you, but you are the little girl he always wanted to have and to love.

Bill's brothers, Jim and Howard...you reminded him of happy childhood days, told him jokes, laughed with him, and prayed for him. You watched in anguish as a horrible disease devastated his body and took away his life. You were the world's best brothers.

Bill's firefighter brothers, Jim Woody, Buster Watson, and Bill Warwick...you interrupted your lives to take Bill out West in order to fulfill a lifetime, and then a dying wish. You blessed his life with your friendship, and you blessed his last days with this one immense act of kindness. He was so grateful. Buster...your detailed account of the western trip made it possible for me to describe an experience that gave so much joy to Bill's last days...Thank you.

Our neighbors and friends, Drama and Del Robeson, and Nancy and Jim Alexander...you sat with Bill many hours during my chemo treatments and you helped me and comforted me after his death. I can never repay your love and kindness.

Reverend and childhood friend, John Holland...you sat with Bill, encouraged him, and prayed with him and for him. Throughout those difficult months, you helped him to renew and deepen his relationship with Christ. I will be grateful beyond forever.

My sisters and brothers...you felt my pain, helped where you could, and you grieved with me from a distance. I always felt your love and compassion.

My niece, Cynthia Enuton...you helped me immeasurably by sharing your insight and knowledge of writing a story, as well as your technical expertise. I am especially grateful for your encouragement and patience.

Brenda and Charlie Weaver...some angels do not have wings, so we call them friends. You have blessed my life with your friendship, and I thank you for being there after the storm.

Pastor Phil Jones and the First Baptist Church of Powell, Tennessee, family...you were faithful in Christian fellowship. You visited us, brought meals, and you obediently and faithfully lifted us up to God in prayer.

Those patients and family members, who shared stories of their own difficult journey with ALS on personal websites...your stories encouraged me and helped me prepare for what was to come. I prayed for you.

The ALS and MD Associations...you provided most of the information and educational materials I so desperately needed in order to care for my husband. You were my lifeline. God bless you in your continued efforts to find answers for this dreadful disease.

Introduction

This is a story about a journey—a journey not anticipated or planned, but a reluctant, miserable voyage brought on by a devastating illness. It is a story I never dreamed I would write; a story one would hope never to have the desire or necessity to read. Some readers may expect to find inspiration or be emotionally uplifted by this story and will be disappointed. What they will find is a true narrative of grim details and events related to a life changing trial that does not have a happy ending. For me and my family, this dreadful and unforeseen journey became a battle against ignorance, uncertainty, fear, despair, misery and suffering, and death. For me as a Christian, it became a ceaseless effort, even a struggle, to understand God's plan and purpose for this terrible trial—this journey through fire.

My husband, Bill, was diagnosed with Amyotrophic Lateral Sclerosis in January of 2003. Extreme grief, dread, and tragedy surrounded us as the disease stalked him unmercifully. It finally defeated him with death after nineteen long months. There were many challenges during our journey. We struggled to accept the inevitable, to understand the disease and its consequences, to find appropriate medical care and treatment, and the daunting undertaking to determine how to access the numerous resources, which would be required for Bill's care. The mental and emotional consequences related to the grief, desperation, helplessness, and then hopelessness were the greatest and most difficult challenges of all.

Amyotrophic Lateral Sclerosis (ALS or Lou Gehrig's disease) is an affliction I would come to know as, "The disease from Hell." At the time of Bill's diagnosis, I had been a practicing RN for forty-five years. I had cared for many people with a wide range of serious or terminal illnesses, and I was more than familiar with suffering and death. However, I knew little about ALS. I could remember only one patient, very early in my career, with an ALS diagnosis. He was in the early stages of the disease and did not appear limited in any way. I recalled from nursing school that it is a relatively rare disease, usually fatal, and with no known cure. Other aspects and facts had long faded from memory. As I began the search for information, it became clear very quickly that the care for someone afflicted with an illness such as this would be complicated. There was a great deal to learn, and I was not prepared. During my daily efforts with Bill's care, especially as the illness progressed, I had my nursing education, experience, and skills to assist me. I wondered how someone with no medical skills or background would ever be able to cope with the enormity of it all. I came to believe that if God showed me the way, lessons learned could equip me to help others who may take a similar journey.

For the person suffering with ALS there are physical disabilities as well as emotional consequences. The caregiver is often in despair; at times not knowing what to do or where to turn for help and support. During my own attempts to provide for Bill's care, I learned that the physician has insufficient time to provide all the education and information required to deal with the devastating effects of the illness.

I learned that many people who work in health care seldom encounter a patient with ALS, and they have limited knowledge of how the disease affects the body. As a result, they do not have an adequate understanding of the various challenges faced by the patient and family. Because of the low incidence of the disease, many physicians may see few if any ALS patients over the lifetime of their practice.

The biblical scripture, and other references to my Christian faith found in this story may conflict with the beliefs and viewpoints of some readers. However, I concluded after much thought and reflection that it would be comforting and helpful to many, and to be untrue to my own convictions and values would be disingenuous at least and cowardly at best. My faith is an integral part of who I am as a person; it did not fail me, but helped me to cope with the turmoil that this disease brought with it. It was the one thing that lifted and carried me through this worst time of my life. As a Christian, I believe God is in control; that our trials and tribulations must first pass through His hands. However, we are not equipped to know or comprehend the mind of God or the reasons behind His purpose. The quest for wisdom in order to see His purpose became a driving force for me.

No one is immune to trials and adversity. All of us are either coming out of a trail, in the middle of a trial, or headed for a trial or some kind of trouble. Many struggle with the age old question, "Why does God allow wounds and suffering?" Perhaps He allows trials to deepen our faith and draw us closer to Him, to destroy self-reliance and lead us to depend on Him more, or to cause us to grow in character and endurance. Our trials may serve to strengthen us so we can help others who go through adversity, or even for the purpose of discipline.

It is difficult for some to acknowledge that God could allow trouble and trials as discipline for wrongdoing. Some may believe that it would be a vengeful and not a loving God who would allow terrible suffering. Whatever the purpose, God is just, and we are reminded, *"For whom the Lord loves He chastens, and scourges every son who He receives." (Hebrews 12:6)*. Nevertheless, He has promised not to allow more than we can actually bear: *"...And God is faithful, He will not let you be tempted (tested) beyond what you can bear," (1Corinthians 10:13).* My own experience in this journey has led me to believe that trials are sometimes allowed to prepare us for future trouble that only God can see; that dreadful trials are sometimes preceded by lesser ones that helps a person to grow in strength and endurance. At first, there may be a light load to test our strength; then a heavier load to test whether or not we can endure. Then eventually for some, comes the heavy, terrible burden that we are sure beyond any doubt that we cannot bear. To this I can relate.

In July of 2000, at a busy intersection, the driver of another car ran a red light striking my car on the driver's side. The strength of the impact forced all the air from my lungs. I was unable to breathe and believed I was going to die. I remember thinking that the actual dying process was not as bad as one imagines. I survived the accident, but it left me with fractured ribs, a fractured pelvis, and many hours of excruciating pain. Several weeks of difficult therapy were required, and I was unable to work. I have always been a careful driver, and I was angry that another person's carelessness could cause me so much misery. Later, I learned that this type of accident, described as a T-bone, is often fatal. In the process of attempting to deal with my pain and anger, I realized that I was fortunate to be alive, and I thanked God for sparing my life.

In December of 2000, a breast mass showed up on a routine mammogram. Prior to the biopsy, I prayed it would not be cancer, but it was. I prayed it would be a non-aggressive cell type, but it turned out to be an aggressive tumor, which tends to spread and reoccur. Most of 2001 revolved around surgery for a mastectomy; then harsh chemotherapy with all the side effects of nausea, weakness, hair loss, and depression. Only those who have experienced breast cancer can identify with the emotional chaos connected to this disease. I prayed often during that time, and I grew closer to God. He did not answer my prayers the way I wanted, but He provided the strength and courage I needed to weather the storm and survive. I recall one particular long and sleepless night when, overwhelmed by dread and fear, I had reached my lowest point both physically and mentally. I prayed desperately just to have peace, and peace came in an instant. My faith flourished that night, for I knew that God was watching. I would soon learn that my own troubles pale in comparison to the unspeakable anguish that was lurking just around the corner.

This is Bill's story, for the suffering belonged to him, as did the courage. The telling of it has not been easy. Many times since his death, I have gathered the information and sat down with the best intentions of putting it all together, but feelings or images would take me back to some sorrowful time or event. The painful memories would cloud my mind and not allow me to continue. The observations, thoughts, feelings, perceptions, and conclusions found in the story are strictly my own, as witnessed from the vantage point of spouse, caregiver, and friend. The journal I kept during Bill's illness provides the verification and chronicle for the pages. Keeping a journal helped me to cope and stay focused on the challenges of caring for someone with such a complicated illness. It helped me to retain a degree of sanity in the midst of the surrounding chaos. The reader will discover that I sometimes faltered and stumbled along the way. I did not always make the best decisions. I put on my nurse's hat more often than I should have, and I wore it too long. The last months of Bill's life were especially trying. I was dealing with my second bout of breast cancer when his illness was having its worst effects on his mind and body. The entire journey was difficult, but the hardest were those last weeks when it became unbearably clear that he was going to die and leave me. I held fast to my faith during those times, and when the darkest hours vanquished any assurance of hope, I held on mightily to God's promises.

Even as Christians, we have contempt for suffering, but when it comes, we have little choice but to bear it. Nevertheless, God is faithful. Reflected in His promises throughout the Bible is the assurance that He will provide whatever is needed to sustain and to overcome adversity. He has not promised a life free of trouble and peril, but He has promised to go with us through the fiery trials. Some who read this story may be in the midst of a tribulation that seems too great—too terrible to bear. They may feel as I did, that God has turned away, gone away, or does not care. Because He has promised, we can be assured that He has not gone, for He cannot and does not lie. It is my desire that what I have learned about this complicated and mysterious illness will help someone else to better understand and face the challenges and turmoil it presents. I trust it may assist to light the way for someone who is caring for a person in a battle against this particular horrendous disease; that something written on these pages will provide some measure of comfort and hope to anyone who may be struggling in the midst of a similar, terrible trial. I pray they will learn as I did, to lean on the power that is greater than any other.

I wrote this story in Bill's memory. Even though the telling of the story has brought back very painful memories and reawakened sadness, grief, and heartache—it has been cleansing for my soul. My finest hope is that it will serve to glorify God who is always present in the midst of the storm.

What God Hath Promised

God hath not promised skies always blue,
Flower-strewn pathways all our life through.
God hath not promised sun without rain,
Joy without sorrow, peace without pain.

God hath not promised that we shall not know,
Toil and temptation, trouble and woe.
He hath not told us that we shall not bear,
Many a burden, many a care.

God hath not promised smooth roads and wide,
Swift, easy travel, needing no guide.
Never a mountain-rocky and steep,
Never a river-turbid and deep.

But God hath promised strength for the day,
Rest for the laborer, light for the way.
Grace for the trials, help from above,
Unfailing sympathy, undying love.

Annie Johnson Flint (1866-1932)

*Blessed be the God and Father of our
Lord Jesus Christ,
the Father of all mercies, and God
of all comfort,
who comforts us in all our tribulations,
that we may be able to comfort those
who are in any trouble,
with the comfort with which we ourselves
are comforted by God.*

2 Corinthians 1:3-4

One

A Pink Marble Stone
Tuesday, February 15, 2005

It is bitter cold in the cemetery today, yet quiet and peaceful. There are no other visitors on the grounds as far as I can see. The wind is harsh, and my jacket is thin—not suited for the weather. All around me there are remnants of morning frost. The grass is brittle and winter brown, and it crackles beneath my feet as I walk. The wind has piled up bunches of left over autumn leaves around the base of the standing monuments and tosses them furiously over the frozen ground. Chimney smoke rises from a few houses that can be seen in the distance, and across the rolling fields of gravestones, I can see a vast array of color in the many flower arrangements that adorn the graves in this well-kept cemetery. Brightly decorated small Christmas trees, wreaths, and other seasonal decorations are scattered here and there. Some are lying on the ground; some are faded and in disarray. It is a dreary place to spend a chilly, wintry morning.

Our burial plots are located in this particular cemetery because Bill came across them years ago in a newspaper ad. As usual, he could not pass up what he considered "a good deal." The burial grounds, established in the early 1900's, contain many age-worn, unique monuments, which stand in the oldest sections of the 135 acres. Many of the inscriptions on the weathered marble are sad yet intriguing to read. The short life spans of the children, engraved on many stones, are especially touching. The two large oak trees near Bill's monument are void of leaves, yet they extend their long branches as if to stand guard in the stillness. His oldest brother, Jim, also has burial plots just a short distance down the winding road. The two older brothers, Jim and Howard, have had various health problems over the years, and Bill would teasingly remind them, "I'm a lot healthier than either of you guys." He never dreamed that his life would end first; that he would be the first to lie here beneath this cold earth.

Today is Bill's birthday. He would have been sixty-nine years old, and I have brought birthday balloons for his gravesite. The three multi-colored, helium-filled balloons had bumped vigorously around the inside of the car as I attempted to remove them. I could imagine Bill laughing at my attempts to hold onto the twisting, turning strings. In spite of my concerted efforts and to my dismay, the swirling wind soon prevailed, and I watched helplessly as two balloons broke away and rushed quickly over the cemetery grounds into the sky. As the last balloon inscribed with, "I love you" was set free, I hoped to see it fly higher than a balloon would normally be able to rise. At first, a swift downdraft caught it, and it collided with one gravestone and then another. My hopes and expectations faded as it headed for a group of tall trees. Suddenly, as if by some guided force, a strong gust of wind grabbed the fluttering object and it began an upward drift. I stood by the roadside and watched the balloon's gradual but steady climb. It soared higher and higher toward Heaven. It finally became but a tiny speck in the pale blue sky. As it finally disappeared from sight I thought, "Surely, God is watching."

Bill's gravestone is easy to find. The unique color of the marble, a deep gray with a dusk-rose tint, causes it to stand out among the other common gray stones. When I first saw the monument following its placement, it occurred to me that he would not approve of the color of the marble and would have preferred something more masculine. Nevertheless, it is a beautiful stone, and there is no remedy for it now. Near Bill's gravesite, there are a few gravestones with unusual names. I remember when Bill and I visited this cemetery in the past; he often made some sort of witty observation about the names on certain stones. He did not intend to be disrespectful of the departed in any way. It was just another opportunity to use his dry but typical sense of humor to make me smile. He had a one-liner about graveyards that he thought was funny. When driving past some graveyard, he would say, "People are just dying to get in that place."

I began to visit Bill's grave soon after his funeral, and I noticed a solitary grave by the roadside. The artificial flowers in the single grave marker's vase were pale and gray in color. They looked as if they had been there for a very long time. Now, when I place new flowers on Bill's grave, I leave some on that grave as well. Each time, I think about this man's family, and I wonder if anyone will bring flowers for our grave after I am gone. When I was growing up, Decoration Day or Memorial Day was a cherished annual custom. It honored those who gave their life for freedom, but it was also for remembering loved ones who had died. We always placed flowers on our family's graves. Today, it is unusual to see people of the younger generation coming to the graveyard for this purpose, and I fear this cherished tradition may be vanishing. I still remember climbing the narrow pathway leading to the small family burial ground in the countryside. The cemetery, on top of a steep hill and surrounded by fields of wildflowers, was just across the road from my grandmother's house. I had not known most of the people whose names I saw inscribed on the weathered stones, but I listened when the grownups recalled memories of loved ones who had died. I heard about my maternal grandfather who died at age forty-two in the line of duty as a county sheriff. I remember seeing the graves of my three stillborn little brothers. Only rocks marked their small graves. I went back to the cemetery a few years ago with my sister Kathleen, and the rocks were still there. Our grandfather's headstone, because it is so aged and worn, had separated from its stone base and fallen over. It had been lying on the ground until we set it back in place.

These old childhood experiences cause recollection of some deeply rooted "Old Wife's Tales" concerning graveyards. These old adages, much like other cherished traditions, tend to pass down from generation to generation. When I was a youngster, children viewed graveyards as very scary places, probably because of the stories and superstitions that children learned very early growing up in the Appalachian Mountains. As I make my way to Bill's gravestone, I recall a few that are fitting for a place such as this. The old folks would tell us that we must always hold our breath when going past a cemetery. Meaning when you breathe, you could inhale the spirit of someone recently buried and end up in the graveyard yourself. They warned, "Never step on a grave." If you do, the spirit of the person buried there would be disturbed. The spirit might later reveal itself as a ghost, or show up in the nighttime to haunt your dreams.

Other customs and mores were less frightening. According to my grandmother it was great luck to find a clover with four leaves in the grass. Searching among the patches of clover could keep us children out of trouble and occupied for hours. If one of us was fortunate enough to see and then make a wish on a shooting star, the wish was bound to come true. I remember gathering with the neighborhood kids on the front porch or in the yard until bedtime. We would gaze up at the stars, waiting with childish anticipation, hoping to see a blazing object streak across the night sky. Mothers and Grandmothers often invented or used these old adages and superstition to provide activities which would occupy their children's mind and time. However, the embellishment of many of the tales over the years caused them to be somewhat laughable. Ridiculous or not, some things learned as a child are obviously tucked away in the subconscious. We sometimes act upon these learned beliefs without conscious thought. As I walk among these graves today, I still find myself being mindful of where I walk—using great care not to step directly on a grave.

The Earth is still bare where they buried the ashes, and the single rose I keep there is still in place. Once again, I notice that the urn burial site seems to be in an odd location. It lies to the left and several feet down from the face of the monument. It is not in line with the headstone, as one would expect. I have been meaning to inquire about this at the cemetery office. My first thought was that the adjoining grave was too close, but then I wondered what real difference it would make if I knew why they buried the urn in that particular spot. As I look upon the small patch of disturbed ground, I am grateful that Bill had insisted on cremation. It is painful to think his poor body could be lying there beneath the cold earth, and I must quickly erase the distressing thought from my mind. I talk to Bill when I visit his grave. I tell him how much I miss him and how lonely my life is without him. My son, John, reminded me one day that dad is no longer here. In my heart, I know what he says is true, but somehow I feel closer to him in the place that holds his earthly remains.

Standing here among these many graves reminds me that the certainty of death and the likelihood of suffering remain mysteries of life that are difficult to comprehend. Each of these stones has its own story to tell; some more tragic than mine. No one can judge, make complete sense of, or know the extent of another person's suffering unless they have walked in their shoes. During my difficult battle with breast cancer, I understood what facing death feels like. I realized my condition could well be fatal, but with treatment I still had hope. Bill had to wake up every day acutely aware that his death was certain. It must have been an unspeakable weight for the heart and soul to bear. My own feelings of emptiness and sorrow are still fresh, and it seems as if it were only yesterday that Bill died. Why did he have to die such a dreadful, cruel death? Why was there not more in the way of medical treatment to help him? Perhaps I do not need to understand, but only to accept that God had a different plan. Sometimes, sorrow eases and peace comes to linger for a while, but grief must be borne by someone. It is during these times, I imagine the Lord must have shifted my grief burden onto His broad shoulders.

It is surreal to see my name and birth date carved onto the left side of the monument—waiting for completion. At first, I anxiously try to avoid looking at Bill's name on the gravestone. However, my eyes soon come to rest on the inscription, William K Knight, February 15, 1936—August 5, 2004. I recall reading somewhere that a wise person once observed, "The short hyphenated space between the birth and death date on a gravestone represents a person's entire lifetime." It is indeed a reminder of the brevity of life. As I stand here by the gravesite, I am struck by a sinking reality. I will not see Bill again this side of Heaven, but I am thankful for the forty-six years we had together. They were many years of caring, sharing, and raising two wonderful children. There were good times and difficult times, happy times and sad times, and times of contentment while growing old together. It all ended too soon.

It is difficult to go on alone and to resume life in this new role as widow. I feel as if I am not the same person. People tell me, that it will get easier with time, but I remain haunted by the despair of the past two years. I relive those dreadful months in thoughts that come in the morning when I wake up, follow me around in the daytime, and put me to sleep at night. I did my best to help Bill live, but my efforts were in vain. My foe was too strong—too formidable. I have some comfort in knowing that his poor, frail body, almost destroyed by a horrific illness, is now free from all wretchedness, pain, and suffering. My heart still agonizes when I remember the misery he had to endure during his desperate struggle with a disease called ALS. Sadly, I remember how it all began.

*Through the Lord's mercies
we are not consumed,
Because His compassions
fail not.*

*They are new every morning;
Great is Your faithfulness.*

Lamentations 3:22-23

Two

The Journey Begins
Sunday, January 19, 2003

Bill intended to watch a ballgame on TV this Sunday afternoon, but it was not long before he was asleep on the couch. His light sleep seems very peaceful, and I think it must be wonderful to be an optimist to such a degree that even the most alarming of difficulties can be set aside for an afternoon nap. That is unless, like me, you are the designated worrier in the family. If I am under duress or worried, I can usually find diversion and relief by keeping busy. I can relieve a great deal of stress quickly by working at the hospital. Cleaning house is also an excellent diversion, but to occupy my time today, I decided to undertake the project of arranging the many accumulated packets of photos in albums. While sorting through the boxes, I came across some old photos of Bill as a child. In one photo, baby Bill is wearing a little girl's dress; he has shoulder length curly hair and a frown on his face. Another photo shows little boy Bill to be two or three years old. He is sitting on a pony sporting a cowboy hat and western style boots, and his expression bears that same frown. In spite of the frown, anyone could tell that he was a beautiful child. These are the only baby photos of Bill, and they remind me of a story his mother told concerning his birth. In the 1930's, babies were seldom born in the hospital. A midwife usually attended the mother, but sometimes the doctor came. Bill was fortunate to have the family doctor attend his birth. The doctor delivered Bill, but was unable to get him to cry or breathe. He turned to Bill's father and remarked, "This child is dead." After this announcement, he wrapped the baby in a blanket and placed it in a basket in the corner of the room. Bill's father, not willing to accept the doctor's opinion, picked Bill up and began to breathe into his mouth and nose. Bill finally gasped and began to breathe on his own. Whenever Bill tells this story, he always attributes the circumstances of his birth to a miracle.

That was long ago, and we are much older now. We are both in our late sixties and retired from our life occupations. In 1990, Bill retired as a firefighter with the rank of captain. After a few months of too much leisure time he became dissatisfied and soon took another full time job with the State Government. I retired in 2000 after a forty-five year career as a registered nurse, but I have continued to work few days a week at the same local hospital. We have two great sons and daughters-in-law, and four precious grandsons who live nearby. We have a wonderful extended family, friends, and neighbors. We have a busy, satisfying, and comfortable life. Five years ago, because of arthritic problems with our knees, we moved from our split-level home to a one-level house in a nearby neighborhood where Bill has long desired to live. The house has a large well-landscaped lawn and lots of shrubbery for him to keep in shape. He can always find an interesting and challenging project to do around the house.

Except for back and shoulder surgery, some arthritis due to aging, and minor illnesses, Bill has been healthy, and he lived in anticipation of a long life. However, for the past year, he has experienced weakness in his arms and hands. We assumed these symptoms were due to an arthritic problem in his neck causing pressure on the nerves. We also noticed that his voice becomes weak at times, especially when he is tired. In the fall of 2002, Bill undertook a project to convert one of our three bay garages into a den. While doing carpentry work, he had difficulty picking up nails and other small objects, and lifting the heavier pieces of building material caused unusual fatigue. He told me about muscle twitching he was having in his upper arms. One day he asked me what I thought was wrong with his hands. I looked and noted unusual sunken areas behind the thumbs on the back of his hands. The muscles appeared to have deteriorated or wasted away. We were both bewildered as we thought about possible causes. We did not yet know enough to realize that we should be alarmed.

While Bill was working on his room, even though it was unusual for him to skip meals, he seldom took time to eat. He was actually pleased that he was quickly losing weight. After several weeks, I finally convinced him to see a physician, but he had already lost 20 pounds. The family doctor was concerned about the symptoms, and he referred Bill to a neurologist. Following an MRI, the specialist concluded that it was not a neurological problem, and he referred him to an orthopedic surgeon for surgery on his neck. The orthopedic specialist informed him that the arthritis in his neck was not the cause of the symptoms, and he mentioned ALS as a possibility. He suggested that Bill see an ALS specialist, and his office staff scheduled an appointment for January 17. I was very troubled, but whenever I expressed my concern Bill would say, "You worry too much." He believed there was nothing seriously wrong with him, but a nagging feeling of dread and fear had crept into my heart and mind.

I have frequent bouts of sinus infection in the wintertime and did not accompany Bill to see the ALS specialist that day, but I was not overly concerned while he was at the doctor's office. The chances of him having ALS were extremely minimal. I felt it would be some non-serious and treatable condition. However, when he returned home in the afternoon, it was obvious by his demeanor that the news was not good, and his worried expression spoke volumes. His face was pale and the tone of his voice somber as he started to tell me what the doctor had said. He began with, "It's much worse than we thought." After the examination, he was taken aback by the doctor's statement, "I hope you are a religious man", as if to prepare him for something more sinister to follow. He went on to say Bill's symptoms were consistent with ALS, but more tests would confirm the diagnosis. He said there was little to offer in the area of treatment and there is no cure. Bill, although an optimist, realizing the seriousness of the doctor's words, asked, "How long will it take this disease to kill me." The doctor told him the average life expectancy is three to five years after the initial diagnosis. He ended by saying there were comfort measures for ALS patients. I wanted specific details about everything the doctor said, but it was obvious the events of the day had a profound effect on Bill because he was unable to clearly recall or describe all the information. I was distraught and heartbroken that he had to receive this earth shattering news alone.

Words are powerful, and they can be devastatingly cruel when spoken with lack of compassion and thought. The doctor's comment, "I hope you are a religious man" was probably unintentional, but I thought it to be flippant and inconsiderate. I lost any respect that I might have had for this physician that day. Many times in my career, I have been witness to the unpleasant task of a physician presenting the patient and family with a dreadful diagnosis or other devastating news. They always used extreme care and kindness when relaying disturbing information. I wondered what prompted this physician to make such an inappropriate, unfeeling, and blunt remark. Perhaps it was his own discomfort with having to tell someone he was going to die. I could not help but visualize a scene where the patient said, "No, I am not religious," and what the doctor would have said in response.

I pulled another group of photos from a packet in the photo box. Among them are some that takes me back to a happier time, but in far too many ways a terrible time. It is a photo of Bill and me, as a much younger couple, sitting on a brick wall on the Statue of Liberty grounds. The majestic Twin Towers of the World Trade Center stands behind us; tall and impressive in the background mist. My sister, Kathleen, her husband, Manuel, and Bill and I enjoyed the long ago trip to New York City. However, the towers are no longer there. In fact, as the New Year of 2003 begins, the whole country is still reeling from the terrorist attacks, which took the towers down, just a little over a year ago (September 11, 2001). The assault reduced the two buildings to a huge pile of twisted rubble. They still lie there today as a stark reminder that every tomorrow is uncertain, and we can never know what the future holds.

I vividly remember the day the towers came down. Bill and I were watching a national TV show in our living room. We watched in horror as the first airliner, and then the second, crashed into the sides of the two buildings. We saw some people leaping from windows to a certain death in order to escape the blazing inferno. It is still difficult to comprehend the enormity surrounding the events of that day. I will remember those horrifying scenes depicting untold injuries, numerous deaths, and vast destruction as long as I live. Over 3,000 people died in New York that day; over 300 of these were firefighters. Bill was especially distraught because of the many firefighter brothers who were lost. He had problems sleeping, and he was sad and depressed for weeks. The three firefighters raising the American flag in the midst of the rubble touched him deeply. After much searching, I found and ordered a poster of the scene from an online poster site. He framed it and hung it in his room, which he managed to complete.

Except for five years when Bill drove the fire chief's car he was a firefighter. He was involved with many dangerous fires over the years. Every time the station bell rang, he and his fellow firefighters placed their lives on the line. Along with their comrades, they faced each blazing inferno and braved the discomfort of the heat, stifling smoke, and the deadly fumes. They were exceedingly dedicated to saving lives and property, and they carried young and old from burning buildings. They were the first to respond to every 911 emergency. I remember my own anxiety every time I heard the familiar wail of a fire truck's siren. At first, I hoped it was not Bill's truck. If it was his truck racing to some fire or accident, I prayed it would not be a dangerous one. I recall one incident in particular when his station answered a call to a filling station. The gas pump had exploded severely burning a nine-year-old boy. The ambulance took the child to a burn hospital in another city, but he did not survive. Bill was unable to free his thoughts of the scene for months—maybe he never did. Being a firefighter's wife, I learned over the years that no matter where the fire station, or in which city they serve, firefighters are always brothers who guard each other's back. I suppose a person would have to know the heart and mind of a firefighter to completely understand their dedication to duty, devotion to each other, and to appreciate why Bill was so distressed after September 11. Bill could identify with the firefighters selfless courage and the danger they faced that day. He knew what it was like to realize that you might have heard the last bell; that you may never see your loved ones again.

When I think about the future and the trials to come, I foresee an unclear pathway---unfamiliar and frightening, and I am faced with a multitude of questions. How does one attempt to comfort someone who has learned they are facing an illness that will eventually bring misery and death? How does one prepare to help relieve the suffering a loved one must bear? How can I ever face the grief, loneliness, and the uncertainty of a future without the person with whom I have shared most of my life? How do we begin to prepare ourselves to deal with the tremendous problems and challenges that lie ahead? I do not yet know the answers to these ominous questions. Since Bill's diagnosis on that fateful day of January 17, 2003, all we are able to do is hold each other and pray. Somehow I know in my heart that this is the beginning of a long and arduous journey.

Jim, Bill, and Howard Knight
Early 1950's

Bill Sr. and Bill Jr.
December, 1960

Shirley and Bill on the Statue of Liberty grounds, New York City 1986

Kathleen (my sister), Shirley and Bill
on the Statue of Liberty grounds, New York City 1986

Then you shall call.
And the Lord will answer;
You shall cry,
And He will say
"Here I am."

Isaiah 58:9

Three

Waiting and Praying
Friday, January 24, 2003

We were blessed with two wonderful sons who now have families of their own. It is painful to see the sorrow on their faces when they learned about their father's illness. Like most people, they understand that ALS is a wretched, fatal disease, but they know little else. It is too soon to reveal all the grim details of what their father is facing. Sweeter memories take me back in time to when they were young and untroubled; when character traits were obvious. Our oldest son, Bill Jr., was originally to be named William Stephen. However, Bill changed the name on his birth certificate to William Kenneth Knight Jr. He failed to discuss the change with me, but it seemed to be important to Bill, so I had no objections. Even when a young child, our Billy's determined personality, much like my own, was obvious. In addition to being sensitive and caring, he still has that head-strong streak today. Our youngest son, John Kelly, is much like his father in looks and temperament. He has that same somewhat devilish personality. While a teenager, Johnny stayed with his grandmother at night for several years so she could continue to live at home. Bill's father had died and she was afraid to stay alone at night. It was a remarkable sacrifice for a young boy.

Bill's two older brothers, Jim and Howard, come by often. When the three are together, they usually reminisce about bygone days, laugh and tell jokes, argue about politics, or give each other a hard time as they did when they were growing up. The three brothers have been close all their lives. There were four children in the family. Their father was a pharmacist and was still working when he died in his seventies. Their mother was a stay-at-home mom devoted to raising her children. Growing up Bill was known to be somewhat mischievous. His brothers always looked after him, but on describing their little brother and recounting his antics would say, "He was a real pain sometimes." Their only sister, Helen, had sustained a head injury during birth. She grew up mentally challenged, and her mother always cared for her at home. Helen was unable to talk, but she was otherwise very healthy. As a child, she learned to roller skate, and she liked to play with dolls. She was intelligent in many ways. She developed her own version of a sign language. Checking her own pulse meant "doctor", and by imitating holding a baby in her arms, she was telling us that someone was expecting. She had a curious and consistent habit that everyone, especially her brothers, thought was amusing. Any shoes, not attached to someone's feet, ended up in a straight row somewhere in the house. While growing up, his sister's unfortunate circumstance was the only real sadness that Bill could recall in his young life.

During Bill's growing-up-years, everybody called him Billy, and by all accounts everyone doted on and spoiled the cute little boy with brown eyes and curly black hair. He attended the community church, rode his bicycle to the local swimming pool, and roller-skated on Minnesota Avenue where many of his relatives resided. Along with his brothers and friends, he played in the surrounding hills and woods. They disobeyed their mother by rope swinging over a deep, dangerous rock quarry. Bill associates his childhood and growing-up-years with happy, adventurous times. Now, when I see him sitting quietly alone and buried in deep thought, I imagine he must be thinking back over his life, and I am grateful that he has happy memories.

Jim and Howard are emotional men, especially where family is concerned. They are broken hearted about Bill's illness. Jim has struggled for years with a disease called Myasthenia Gravis. In Myasthenia Gravis, the body's immune system attacks its own tissues, but what triggers the autoimmune response is unclear. The attack occurs at the junction between nerve and muscle, which results in fatigue and weakness of voluntary muscles—muscles we can control, such as arm and leg movement. There are tests to confirm a diagnosis for Myasthenia Gravis and there are medications for treatment. Most people with this disease can expect to live a normal or near normal life.[1] So far, several medications seem to be working to control Jim's symptoms. ALS, on the other hand, is a neurodegenerative or motor neuron disease where the nerves degenerate and die. ALS also affects voluntary muscles. I believe it is unusual for two brothers, with no known family history, to become afflicted with such similar diseases. It causes me to wonder if there could be some genetic connection.

Many friends have called expressing concern. Several of Bill's close friends are especially distressed and desire information. But Bill says he is not ready to have visitors except for the family, and he does not feel like talking to people on the phone. He tells me, "I have to get everything straight in my mind." I know he is thinking about how to interact with other people, how others will perceive him, and if they will treat him differently. I am sure he will not want sympathy or pity. When we are alone, he remains quiet and thoughtful. Even when I question, he refuses to share his feelings, and I can only imagine his unrelenting emotional torture. He voices hope at times by saying, "Everything will be alright." Other times, I see him sitting in his recliner staring into space. He tells me the twitching in his arms has diminished, but I wonder if this is indeed true, or if he is only desperately searching for some small ray of hope.

Worsening leg cramps have been robbing Bill of sleep for several months, but the cramps have been less this week, and he has been able to get more rest. As I have grown older, with all the accompanying aches and pains, sleep for me does not come easy at best. Recently, I dread to see bedtime approaching. Each night, while attempting to sleep, my thoughts become turbulent, race in all directions, and take me to very sinister places. The lack of sleep leaves me exhausted and sometimes makes for an unpleasant day's work at the hospital, but I am thankful for work. Being able to share information about ALS with others in the medical profession adds to my storehouse of knowledge. Sharing my concerns with friends at work seems to lighten the weight of my burden—if only temporarily. Caring for the patients and their problems allows me, if but for a while, to forget the wretched feelings of dread and fear that have become my constant companion. On days that I am not working or looking after a grandchild, my thoughts often race ahead to the coming months and to the challenges that I will need to face in order to provide for Bill's care. I know he will need special equipment and supplies, but are the bathroom doors wide enough for a wheelchair. What problems will we encounter for transport to and from the doctors' offices? As swallowing problems worsen, what foods can I prepare that he will be able to eat? Will we need to consider a move to a house more suitable for handicap people? Will everything he needs be covered by our medical insurance? There are so many perplexing and unanswered questions. The long-term care insurance policies that we purchased approximately five years ago provide much needed consolation.

There is also concern about Bill's current occupation. His job as a manufactured housing inspector is physically demanding. It requires a lot of walking and climbing. He must climb into attics and onto rooftops of the houses he inspects, and I wonder if he is strong enough. He is required to drive a great deal, and he must go out of town often on long and overnight trips. Under the best of circumstances these trips are sometimes exhausting. In addition, he must write in order to fill out multiple forms and numerous reports with hands that no longer serve him properly. Currently, with diligence, he is able to fulfill all the duties of the job, but I anticipate a time when this type of work and any other job endeavor will be impossible. Work has always been an important and gratifying part of Bill's life. I am afraid when he has to stop working altogether, the complete and powerful impact of this tragedy will hit him full force.

I can say with confidence that Bill is a Christian, but he has never been one who cared to discuss spiritual issues. One day unexpectedly he said, "I don't know how I should pray." His comment led me to believe he needed to talk to someone who could counsel with him about his spiritual concerns. I immediately thought of a Baptist minister, John Holland, whom I knew from his visits at the hospital. I was aware that Bill and John had grown up together, and they have been friends since childhood. They lived in the same neighborhood and attended the same church and neighborhood schools. I believed Bill was close enough to John that he could confide in him and be able to tell him what was on his heart. I called John and told him about Bill's illness. He readily agreed to come and see Bill, and he prayed with me on the phone. He promised to pray for Bill and reminded me of God's unrelenting love for us.

Many people are praying for Bill, including family, friends, and neighbors. Several church groups are offering special prayers on his behalf. When people we know learn about his situation, they attempt to offer words of hope and reassurance. They are often at a loss as to what to say. Most people have never known anyone with ALS, so they can only imagine the dreadfulness of the trial we are facing. I often find myself having to explain to people how the disease affects the body; that it is eventually fatal. I also pray for Bill. My fervent prayer is that God will provide His healing touch; that He will reach down and make it all disappear.

Bill relaxing at the Fire Station
Late 1970's

"Fear not, I am with you;
Be not dismayed, for I am your God.
I will strengthen you,
Yes, I will help you,
I will uphold you with My righteous
right hand."

Isaiah 41:10

Four

A Dreadful Diagnosis
Thursday, January 30, 2003

There are no words to express how it feels when your world is crumbling; when every day you wake up to a new and horrifying reality. You would assume that someone who has worked in a hospital for many years could tolerate tragedy, or at least not surprised by it. During my long nursing career, I have witnessed every kind of heartbreak caused by illness, accident, or death. Memories and visions of those experiences are still very clear in my mind. I remember the young soldiers in the Army hospital who had to be cared for on metal frames due to paralysis from the neck down. Their lives were changed forever. While working in the Intensive Care Unit, I witnessed every kind of tragedy imaginable. I can still see the beautiful faces of the children who died following open-heart surgery. Open-heart surgery was not cutting-edge in the 1960's. I can still visualize one of the heart surgeons sleeping in a vacant ICU bed because he would not leave his small patient's side. One never forgets the misfortune of others, but when tragedy comes close to home and touches a loved one, it can cause mental and emotional grief unlike anything else.

Bill had an appointment for nerve testing today, and being the eternal optimist he said, "Don't worry, the tests will be negative." My concern was not the muscle weakness but the muscle twitching; one of the most suspicious symptoms. According to what I have read, this type of muscle twitching indicates nerve destruction and points to ALS. I learned that the diagnosis of ALS can be difficult because there are other diseases and conditions with many of the same symptoms. Most tests and procedures focus on ruling out diseases that mimic ALS, and there are several tests used to assist to establish an ALS diagnosis. I am familiar with the majority of these tests.

An EMG (electromyography), with needle electrodes placed into the muscle, measures the activity of the muscles and the nerves that control them. With an NCV (nerve conduction velocity), the electrode patches are placed on the skin, and an electrical impulse is used to measure the strength and speed of nerve signals. An MRI (magnetic resonance imaging) produces detailed images of the brain and spinal cord in order to test for damage or abnormality. If someone is expected to have, or is diagnosed with ALS, it is important to seek a second opinion from an ALS expert. The expert should be a physician who has a medical specialty in the diagnosis and treatment of ALS patients. If the attending physician cannot recommend someone for a second opinion, you can find a list of certified ALS centers and ALS specialists on the ALS Association website (www.alsa.org).[1]

I met Bill's neurology specialist today. Soon after we arrived at the office, he ushered us into a small room with a tall cot, a computer, and various items of testing equipment. I was able to sit in the room and observe. I watched the doctor's facial expression carefully as he conducted the nerve studies. I suppose I was hoping to see evidence that might provide some blessed reassurance. However, he remained professional and reserved throughout the testing which lasted over an hour. His stern expression let me know he would not be receptive to any questions I might desire to ask. Bill, with his usual dry sense of humor, is able to poke fun at even the most serious of situations. As he lay there on the exam table, connected to all the wires and electrodes, he made amusing remarks about the test, the doctor, and other things related to this experience. A few times, I had to remind him to be quiet and co-operate with instructions. I am sure the joking is a cover-up for all the anxiety he is feeling. As for me, I sought no diversion, but my eyes concentrated on the doctor's face and on the computer screen. The test information, displayed in unfamiliar script, made it impossible for me to make sense of what I was seeing.

When the tests were completed, the doctor spent some time going over the results. He finally turned to Bill with a stern look on his face. I felt a cold wave of apprehension sweep over me as I heard him say, "Mr. Knight, I'm terribly sorry, but I'm 99.5 percent sure you have ALS." He went on to verify that there is no treatment for the disease, and he was not aware of any current clinical trials. For the first time, I could sanction the doctor's previous statement, "I hope you are a religious man." I watched as the color drained from Bill's face. His hopeful expression changed to one of shock and disbelief. The doctor's words had erased all the hope he held in his heart. He made some comment regarding his expectations that the tests were going to be negative. After that, he sat quietly with a downcast expression. He spoke only when asked a direct question.

I knew in my heart the news would be grim, but I had not fully accepted it. I do not recall a great deal about the remainder of the visit. We were ushered into a small, nondescript examination room. The doctor sat down on a stool and explained the test results. He went on to reveal some of the horrifying aspects of the disease, but we were both too stunned to listen to everything he had to say. His demeanor was matter of fact without compassion or words of empathy. When the visit ended, he picked up his Dictaphone, then proceeded to ignore us while dictating mostly in medical terms. When the dictation was completed, I asked about a second opinion. With some hesitation, he said if we thought it was necessary to get a second opinion, he would recommend an ALS specialist located in a nearby state. He told us it could be two months before we could arrange an appointment. He felt sure this doctor would confirm his diagnosis. Bill responded, "I'm not sure I want a second opinion." He told the doctor he wanted to think about it. Still in a state of shock, we somehow found our way back to the parking garage. We drove home in painful silence.

On the way home, I was unable to free my thoughts of the doctor's description of what happens to a person afflicted with ALS. The horror of the situation was becoming a dark image in my mind. I could not believe this could be happening to Bill, but I realized that what we had learned today about his future would change our lives forever. Most of us take our health for granted until illness strikes. In spite of the demands placed on the body and the abuse it sometimes receives, we expect our vital functions to continue to work to keep us going. The human body has amazing powers to fend off disease, fight disease when it happens, and repair itself. What goes awry with a disease such as this? What happens to cause the body to turn on itself with such disastrous consequences? I searched my brain to try to remember more about the physiology of the nervous system, but my recall was scarce. My nursing specialty and expertise was in cardiac care for more than 30 years. One tends to disregard information about illnesses they do not see every day. It is a fact that all body systems are vulnerable and subject to disease and injury. Considering the complexity and intricate balance required for all organs and tissues to work together to sustain life, it is a tribute to the Creator that anyone remains free of disease for long.

I am just beginning to understand this disease and the devastating effects it will have on our lives; especially on Bill as a person. He has been blessed with good looks since he was a young man. Some people have even described him as handsome. He inherited his mother's olive complexion and brown eyes. The gray streak in his black hair began to appear in his late teens. Of course, his hair has since turned entirely white, but he still takes pride in every aspect of his appearance. I cannot help being concerned when I consider how the effects of this disease will influence or alter his self-perception. One consistent aspect of his character is being well dressed. When he was in high-school, he would save his lunch money to buy articles of clothing. After we were married, he never allowed me to iron his shirts because the results did not meet his expectations, and he always sent his trousers to the laundry for creasing. Considering the pride he takes in his appearance, I can only imagine his despair as the muscles deteriorate and his body begins to deform and change. If the course of the illness follows in the same manner as in the majority of cases, Bill is facing an unspeakable trial, and I will be witness to his progression from a healthy, active person to someone who will be unable to move or speak my name. The sadness, distress, and sometimes anger that I feel in my heart are overwhelming. I recognize my anger as a normal process of grief, but it occupies my thoughts making it difficult to pray. I yearn to be positive and hopeful, but considering there is little treatment and no cure for this horrible illness, my hope is quickly fading. I have a troublesome feeling that the second specialist will indeed confirm the ALS diagnosis.

Sometimes, when a person has a serious illness, others often think of them only in terms related to the illness. We tend to forget the special individual who existed before the disease or condition took center stage. When I think of Bill, I see a loving and steadfast person who has a family, a job, dreams, and aspirations; someone with a past and a lifetime of memories. It is my desire that those who read this story will not picture Bill only in terms of the illness that dominates his life, but that they will perceive him as a unique individual who is struggling with a terrible disease. As I consider the immediate future and the difficulties that are sure to come, I think about our children, grandchildren, and our extended family; I think about the sorrow and trouble in store for all the people that I love.

Bill Jr., and Sean, Papaw and John Morgan,
John and Andrew, and Justin
Spring 2001

For the mountains shall depart
And the hills be removed,
But my kindness shall not depart from you,
Nor shall my covenant of peace be removed…

Isaiah 54:10

Five

The Mystery Affliction
Sunday, February 2, 2003

Bill received the ALS diagnosis in the early afternoon on a cold and dreary day in mid January of 2003. Later that night, after Bill had gone to bed, I sat down at the computer and entered ALS into the search engine. I was ill prepared for the horror and unbelievable gloominess that greeted me. My heart raced with anxiety as I scrolled down the screen and began to read and attempt to make sense of what lay before my eyes. I was shaken by the information that described the ravaging effects the disease can have on a person's body. As the facts emerged, it did not take long for me to understand that this was no ordinary disease, but an exceedingly ruthless and deadly affliction. I have experienced fear before but never such a terrible all consuming panic. The fear's cold wave began in my feet and swept upward until it engulfed my entire body, and I felt as if I could not breathe. At that moment, I told the Lord that I would not be able to manage the disease and Bill's care on my own; I asked Him to help me and show me the way. This was only the beginning of many requests and prayers that I would offer up on Bill's behalf in the months to come.

An overwhelming amount of information described the disease in grim detail. I reviewed the Greek meaning of the long medical name, Amyotrophic Lateral Sclerosis. The "A" in Amyotrophic indicates no or negative, "myo" pertains to muscle, and the last syllable "trophic" refers to nourishment (no muscle nourishment). In other words, voluntary muscles do not receive the nerve signals needed to make them function correctly. These specific motor nerve signals travel from the brain along the side or "lateral" edges of the spinal cord. Sclerosis refers to the hardening or scarring, which occurs on portions of the spinal cord due to death of the nerve cells.[1] In the United States, Lou Gehrig's disease is the most common name for ALS. Lou Gehrig was a famous New York Yankees baseball player. In an event at Yankee Stadium on May 2, 1939, he announced a sudden end to his career. He was not playing well, and he knew something was physically wrong. A few months later, he received an ALS diagnosis. He survived only two years following the diagnosis.[2]

There is a great deal of information on the internet about ALS. Most of the websites have references and links relating to additional resources. The ALS Association (ALSA) and Muscular Dystrophy Association (MDA) websites were the most helpful. The ALS Association has a wealth of information in the form of books, manuals, newsletters, and videos, which are available to order. There are links relating to care giving resources for equipment, supplies, and product aids for daily living. You can find the locations of ALS and MD agencies, local clinics, support groups, and other resource agencies for patients and families. There is also information relating to research, clinical trials, and much more. I believe Devine intervention led me to the ALS website. The educational information, which I requested and received from them, is the source of most of what I have learned about ALS. This organization has been my lifeline.

The brain, spinal cord, and the billions of nerve cells make up the nervous system of the human body. This exceedingly complex system can only be touched on in simple terms. Our brain is like a central computer that controls all bodily functions. The brain communicates with the body through the spinal cord and an enormous network of nerves, which branch out from the cord to every body system and organ. Nerves (neurons) are like a network of electrical wires that carry messages and information back and forth between the brain and all parts of the body. It is amazing to learn that these nerve impulses travel at a speed of more than 200 miles an hour. The brain uses the information it receives from the nerves to coordinate all the bodily actions and reactions.[3] The nervous system is at work when we think, remember, learn, laugh, cry, sing, sleep, dream, move, touch, write, or feel pain or pleasure, etc. We would not be able to do anything, or even exist, without the functions of the nervous system.

There are many kinds of nerves. Specific nerves (neurons) are involved in each and all of our bodily functions—in walking, talking, eating, breathing, heartbeat, vision, hearing, etc. Motor neurons are muscle controlling nerve cells. They reach from the brain to the spinal cord and from the spinal cord to the muscles. These specialized nerves provide for voluntary muscle movement and muscle power. In other words, they tell the muscles what to do. These motor neurons are at work when we voluntarily reach for an object, walk up the stairs, or operate a computer using our hands. The heart and digestive system are also made of muscle, but they are under involuntary muscle control. For example, we cannot voluntarily control our heartbeat or the digestive system processes.[4]

ALS is a disease of the nervous system affecting motor neurons. In ALS, there is a progressive degeneration of the motor neurons gradually leading to nerve cell death. The exact cause is unknown. As the nerves die, the muscles powered by the nerves become weak and non-functioning. Muscle weakness is progressive, occurring gradually but steadily over time. The disease progression eventually results in widespread muscle deterioration. In the later stages of the disease, muscle weakness can lead to paralysis and respiratory failure.[5] ALS rarely affects the mind and mental abilities. It does not directly affect muscle function under involuntary control such as digestion and bowel function. The disease does not generally affect the senses of sight, smell, touch, hearing, and taste. Other areas not affected are sexual function and the internal organs (heart, liver, kidneys, etc.). The rate of disease progression can vary from person to person, and it can be slow, moderate, or rapid. The moderate or average rate of disease progression and survival is three to five years following diagnosis. There are various treatments, which a person may choose to lengthen their life beyond the usual course of the illness.[6]

Symptoms of ALS can vary widely from person to person. Early symptoms, such as tripping or dropping things, are so slight they can go unnoticed at first. As the illness progresses, the person may experience weakness in the fingers, hands, arms, and legs. Other symptoms may include slurred or thick speech, muscle stiffness, poor coordination, weight loss, muscle cramps, twitches under the skin (fasciculation), shortness of breath, and difficulty swallowing. The progressive muscle weakness eventually begins to hinder physical mobility. The afflicted person may begin to have problems performing activities of daily living—walking, moving about, self-care, speaking, chewing, and eating.. As the weakness and paralysis continues to spread, it can affect the diaphragm and other muscles that assist breathing. A respiratory crisis occurs when these muscles can no longer make the lungs function to exchange air. At some point, a decision about whether to accept permanent ventilator support will be required in order for the person to survive.[7]

There are two types of ALS. In Sporadic ALS (SALS), the disease just happens with no known reason. Sporadic ALS accounts for 90-95 percent of cases. An inherited, abnormal gene is the cause of Familial ALS (FALS), and the person will have other family members who have had the disease. Familial ALS accounts for 5-10 percent of cases. It is important to remember that the rate at which the disease progresses and the sequence and pattern of progression can vary widely in different individuals. There is no difference in symptoms and disease progression whether Sporadic or Familial ALS.[8] The average life expectancy for ALS is three to five years, but many people live five, ten, or more years. The common age of onset is between ages forty and seventy. A small number of people diagnosed with ALS experience a halting or slowing of disease progression. The number of new cases each year in the US is two per 100,000 population, with as many as 30,000 having the disease at any given time. There are nearly 120,000 cases diagnosed worldwide each year (328 new cases each day).[9] There are no treatments available to stop or cure ALS, and only one drug (Rilutek) approved for use in the disease. Most treatments focus on managing the symptoms, providing comfort, and developing and making the necessary resources available, which will allow ALS patients to live with as much quality of life as possible. Education for the patient, family, and caregivers is a tremendously important aspect of patient care.[10]

ALS has quickly taken complete control over our lives, and I am attempting to educate myself to prepare for Bill's care. I search the internet for information about ALS when he is not at home because his behavior indicates that he may be in denial and not prepared mentally or emotionally to understand or accept what it all means. I came to this conclusion because he seldom talks about the illness, and he does not ask questions or attempt to search for information on his own. Sometimes, I wonder if he has adequate perception of just how serious this life-threatening situation could be. On a few occasions, I printed information about the disease from various internet websites, which I thought would be important for him to know. He reluctantly and briefly skimmed over the first few pages, and then would lay it aside. His response being, "I'll read it later", or "I don't feel like reading it right now." I do not know if he ever read any of the material. Maybe if he has to learn about the disease, he will have to come nearer to some phase of acceptance. It is obvious that he is not yet ready. A gradual realization of these facts lets me know that I am the one who must learn everything possible about this horrific disease and its consequences. In the meantime, I will continue to hope and pray for healing.

He Keeps the Key

Is there some problem in your life to solve,
Some passage seeming full of mystery?
God knows who brings the hidden things to light.
He keeps the key.
Is there some door closed by the Father's hand
Which widely opened you had hoped to see?
Trust God and wait, for when He shuts the door,
He keeps the key.
Is there some earnest prayer unanswered yet,
Or answered not as you thought 'twoud be?
God will make clear His purpose by-and-by.
He keeps the key.
Unfailing comfort, sweet and blessed rest,
To know of every door He keeps the key,
That He at last, when just He knows 'tis best,
Will give the key to thee.

Author unknown

*Blessed is the man who perseveres
under trial, because when he has
stood the test, he will receive
the crown of life that God
has promised to them
who love Him.*

James 1:12 (NIV)

Six

Is God Watching?
Tuesday, February 11, 2003

February 15th will be Bill's sixty-seventh birthday. When I brought up the subject he said, "It will probably be the last one?" Considering how he feels, I have been in a dilemma as how to proceed as if all is normal; that our world is not really falling apart. The uncertainty of learning to live with Bill's ALS diagnosis has helped me to realize that the ongoing mental and emotional effects of the illness can invade, influence, and alter every aspect of a person's life. After much soul-searching, not yet willing to allow the disease to have complete control, I decided that it was important for Bill to plan to live. Therefore, I chose not to agonize about or deviate from my usual approach to his birthday. We usually get together with our two sons and the grandchildren and celebrate with a family dinner, birthday cake, and gifts. Because Bill appreciates being well dressed, the boys and I usually give him clothes. However, he is so particular about what he wears; I prefer that he go along to assist in choosing the specific and desired items of clothing for my gift. So far, he has been resistant to my efforts to convince him to go shopping with me.

Yesterday, Bill finally agreed to participate in a shopping trip, more or less to appease me, but it was clear that he was not looking forward to it. While walking through the men's section of a local department store, the manikins displayed a pleasing assortment of well-coordinated outfits. He looked at a few items, but it was obvious he was disengaged. At last he said, "I don't know why I'm looking at these clothes?" Followed by, "I will have no need for more clothes." With those words, he absolutely refused to purchase anything for himself. I could imagine what he must be thinking. He must be considering that he will lose more weight and the clothes will no longer fit, or more than likely he doubts he will be around to wear them. Understanding his feelings, I did not try to persuade him to reconsider the clothing. However, I did convince him to help me choose a pair of pajamas in case he should need them for a hospital stay. He usually wears a size large but due to his weight loss, I chose a medium size. He quickly reminded me, "I will be lucky to fit into a size small when this disease is through with me." I soon learned that those words were indeed accurate and a prophecy of what was soon to come. I happened to be in the bedroom when Bill stepped from the shower one morning. The disease has already transformed his body, and I was astonished at the marked muscle deterioration. He is thin all over, but the muscles in his legs and buttocks especially show the increased muscle wasting described in the text. While helping him to button his shirt, I noticed the muscles twitching in his upper arms. I now recognize it as a sign that more nerves are in the process of destruction. He tells me he has experienced this same twitching sensation in his tongue; another symptom pointing to ALS.

Learning about ALS has prompted me to be more observant of all of Bill's symptoms. He has the described weakness in his hands, arms, and fingers. I have noticed that his breathing seems labored at night. He sleeps restlessly, and sometimes his entire body will make an abrupt, jerking movement. It is so forceful it wakes me from a deep sleep. If this is an ALS symptom, it is new and unusual. It occurs to me that Bill has had some symptoms for months, which could be due to ALS. His speech was somewhat slurred at times, and he would choke on food more often than what seemed to be normal. This past year, I noticed he would become short of breath while doing yard work or other types of exertion causing activity. If I expressed concern, he would assure me by commenting, "I wish you wouldn't worry about my breathing." He said his lung problems are due to all the years of smoke inhalation when he was a firefighter. He has had medical treatment for restless legs and legs cramps in the past. Recently, the leg cramps have worsened in frequency and intensity, and he now has foot cramps. All of these symptoms are ominous and telling.

Last week was a sad and trying week. Bill has been unable to sleep and is constantly tired. The mental turmoil he is experiencing is obvious as he attempts to come to terms with his dreadful situation. He appears restless during the day. He frequently paces the floor, goes from room to room, or takes frequent trips to the garage. We reported these problems to the family physician during Bill's visit last Friday. The doctor prescribed a different medication for restless legs as well as a sleeping pill, and he has slept better the past few nights. He rides the exercise bike a couple of times a day, and he consistently performs arm and leg exercises in an attempt to strengthen his weakening muscles. My heart breaks as I watch his determined efforts; efforts I fear will be useless in altering the course of this terrible illness.

At the mention of food, Bill's standard comment is, "I'm not hungry." He drinks high protein supplements hoping to gain strength and maintain his weight, but it continues to decline, and he is easily fatigued. H does not understand that the muscle wasting contributes to the weight loss. His face is thinning and his eyes are sunken with dark circles. He has traversed quickly from a healthy appearing man to someone who is obviously not well. Even though the doctor informed Bill that he was 99.5 percent sure of the ALS diagnosis, he is still hanging onto hope and expecting some recent blood tests to be negative. He thinks the doctor will change his opinion. I believe the blood tests are irrelevant, but I keep my doubts to myself.

On Saturday, Bill went to watch our grandson, John Morgan, play basketball at his school. On his return home, he seemed sad and depressed. On my questioning, he said it is difficult to be around people who know that he has this disease. He told me, "People I've known for a very long time avoided talking to me tonight." I reminded him that most people are uncomfortable in these situations and do not know what to say, so they will avoid and say nothing. Saturday afternoon we baby-sat with our youngest grandson. Andrew is three years old. He is a precious, active little boy who has red, curly hair. As Bill held him on his lap he said, "This little guy will not remember me when I am gone." He worries that the boys will be frightened of him when he becomes what he refers to as, "A vegetable."

Bill has never been interested in discussing end of life issues, but I am just the opposite. I have to have everything in place. In the past, because he preferred not to deal with it, he has left the task of obtaining living will and durable power of attorney documents up to me. Our documents are fifteen years old, and I thought they might need to be revised or redone. Our living will contains a clear statement. It says that if either of us should have a terminal condition, and there is no reasonable expectation for recovery; that the condition (as a medical probability) would result in death, we would not want our dying to be artificially prolonged. We talked about some of the artificial means commonly used to prolong someone's life such as CPR (Cardiopulmonary Resuscitation), feeding tubes, and breathing assistance by means of a ventilator. After the discussion he told me, "I'm not sure if I would agree to a feeding tube, but I am sure I don't want to live on a ventilator." He told me he is sorry for all the stress and burden his illness has placed on me.

Bill usually avoids discussing spiritual or faith based issues, and I am the one who usually initiates the subject. Because the illness he has is fatal, he must have many profound questions or concerns that he is unwilling or unable to put into words. Does he question as to why this illness occurred if God is loving and merciful? Just recently he commented, "God may be punishing me," and he expresses guilt for not having lived a better Christian life. I reminded him that all people suffer tribulation; that awful things happen to good and bad alike; even to the most devote Christians. Sometimes, my own faith waivers, and I am also attempting to understand the purpose for this trial. Why did this illness have to strike this good caring person? Sometimes, my heart is so heavy it is impossible to pray, and my mind fills with deep despair, "Has God abandoned us at a time when we need Him most?"

Bill's friend, Reverend John Holland, came by the house last Tuesday to visit. The two of them seemed to have an enjoyable time reminiscing about bygone days. John spoke of tragedies that he had experienced in his own life, and he had questioned God as to why. He said that although he is spiritually prepared, like most people, he does not want to die. Later that night, Bill told me he was grateful to John for helping to clear up some of the troublesome spiritual issues he had been grappling with. He has been praying that the illness would be taken from him. When healing did not occur, he had questioned as to why his prayers went unanswered. He has been concerned that questioning God is an indication that his faith is not strong. John provided reassurance by saying, "God understands our questioning." I will always thank God for John Holland. Bill does not want his body to be buried in the ground, and has always said he prefers cremation when he dies. He went so far as to purchase cremation burial policies. I have been somewhat uncertain about cremation because I did not know if it conflicted with the Baptist faith. I was relieved to hear John say that the Baptist faith held no objections to cremation. Before John left Bill ask him if he would conduct his funeral, and John readily agreed to do so. I was surprised that Bill is able to discuss these necessary but dismal issues this soon. It is obvious that he has given his situation a great deal of thought.

At our age, and even with better knowledge and wisdom of life's misfortunes, the reality as to why we must travel through valleys of darkness remains bewildering, especially where family is concerned. Neither of us has been immune to family tragedy. Bill told me about a young uncle who died with bone cancer. He was only seventeen, and his death was devastating for the entire family. I have always been perplexed as to why my oldest brother, Kenneth, had to die in the prime of his life. I will never forget receiving the heartbreaking news. He was working out of town at the time, and the exact cause of his death remains a mystery to this day. My brother was 38 years old, and he left behind a beautiful wife and five wonderful little girls. I never knew him to be a religious person, so I really had no way of knowing where he would spend eternity. I remember hoping and praying at the time that my brother was spiritually prepared to die. The memories surrounding his death are still painful and they haunt me to this day. The loss of her precious, oldest son was especially heartbreaking and devastating for my mother. She was never the same.

Yesterday I was scheduled for duty at the hospital. Over the years, I have worked in every clinical areas of this hospital, but I finally settled in cardiac care where I was a nurse manager for many years. The last ten years of employment, I worked in the cardiac rehabilitation department. Following retirement, I have continued to work there as many days as I wish and providing they need me. Teaching patients about heart disease is the primary duty of the cardiac rehab nurse in the hospital setting. The patients generally are recovering from some sort of heart disease, including heart attacks and coronary artery bypass surgery. Remaining hopeful is an important part of their recovery. However, because of my own heart's burden, attempting to be positive while talking to the patients and families is difficult. Many of my co-workers are aware of Bill's diagnosis, and they attempt to offer words of hope and encouragement, but I am frequently downcast and on the verge of tears.

One of the Sisters came by one day and talked to me for a while about Bill, and she prayed for us there in my office. It was a beautiful but humble prayer that renewed my hope. She said all the nuns at the convent were offering special prayers for Bill, and she gave me a crucifix to bring to him. It was to be a reminder, because of the cross; that Christ understands his suffering. Before Bill went to bed last night, I gave him the crucifix. He did not speak as he took it in his hand. He looked at it for a short while, and then placed it in an upright position on the table beside his recliner. After that, he never referred to the cross specifically, but I never moved it from where he placed it. I hope it brought him comfort and peace in the difficult and dismal days, weeks, and months that were to come. I also seek comfort, and one does not have to read very far in the pages of this book to conclude that I appreciate old inspirational poetry. I can find much consolation in the lines of verse, but my major source of comfort and solace lies in the words of scripture. It seems beyond all human comprehension that as believers we can have the assurance of the constant presence of God; that He is always with us.

"Where can I go from Your Spirit? Or where can I flee from Your presence? If I ascend into Heaven, You are there; If I make my bed in hell, behold, You are there. If I take the wings of the morning, and dwell in the uttermost parts of the sea, even there Your hand shall lead me, and Your right hand shall hold me." (Psalm 139: 7-10)

Andrew and Papaw Bill, 2001

Cast your burden on the Lord,

and He shall sustain you;

He shall never permit the

righteous to be moved.

Psalm 55:22

Seven

Searching for Hope
Wednesday, February 12, 2003

When trouble shows up on your door-step, the old adage, "Holding onto Hope," takes on a more profound meaning. My mother had a strong capacity for hope. She was in her early seventies when she was diagnosed with esophageal cancer. The doctor said the non-filtered cigarettes she had smoked for many years were probably the cause. She came to stay with me during her treatment. She had surgery at the hospital where I worked, and I helped her choose a surgeon to perform the difficult operation. He was the same caring, Christian doctor who had slept in the ICU beside his patients. She survived a grueling surgery, radiation, chemotherapy, and many months of distress and pain. The cancer finally invaded her brain, and it ended her life a little over a year following the surgery. I used to go by her hospital room after work to sit with her for a while. I can still picture her lying in the hospital bed with her baldhead covered by one of the turbans she preferred to wear. She had such a difficult life. I remember thinking that it seemed unfair that she should have to endure so much pain and suffering at the end. My mother never had a great deal in the way of material things. She always put her children first if there was extra money to spend. She seemed to be happy with the simple pleasures of life. While she was in the hospital, I kept a supply of her favorite orange slice candy by her bedside. She was unable to tolerate food, but she could always nibble on this old-fashioned confection. I still think of her every time I see orange-slice candy in a store. She held onto hope until those last weeks when she asked me, "How long does it take cancer to kill a person?" I knew then, that whatever earthly hope she was clinging to had vanished.

Hope is a fragile, yet all-consuming human trait that keeps us going when the odds are stacked against us. It is that longing or expectation that things will get better, which pushes us to keep trying and go forward into an uncertain tomorrow. Human beings have a capacity for hope because a sustaining power is needed to help us manage adversity and tribulation. However, the hope that helps us deal with life's troubles and trials can be fleeting, and we often find ourselves in the midst of despair—not knowing where to turn. We cannot live without earthly hope, but we need a deeper hope; one that will last forever. The Lord offers an eternal hope that lifts and sustains when night closes in and darkness dims the way. Death cannot destroy this blessed assurance of hope. However, I am not yet ready to give up on earthly hope for Bill. It is this hope, which compels me to continue to search for answers.

The ALS Association lists some theories about possible causes of motor neuron degeneration. Glutamate is a special chemical the nerves must have in order to connect or communicate with each other. Too much glutamate can be toxic to the nerve cells. Finding drugs that will reduce the amount of this chemical substance has been one aim of research. Rilutek, the one drug approved for ALS, is a glutamate inhibitor (it blocks the release of glutamate). A possible link between viruses and ALS has been a focus of research study in the past. Several investigators have revealed some evidence for the possible role of inflammatory response in ALS, but inflammation can result from numerous causes. There are some suggestive findings, which points to environmental factors that might influence the development of ALS, but there is still no conclusive evidence.[1]

In a recent study, a comparison was made between soldiers who were deployed to the Gulf war region and soldiers who were not deployed. Early results of the research indicated a higher than normal incidence of ALS in veterans who served in that war.[2] In the 1950's an extraordinarily high occurrence of ALS was discovered in Guam and the Trust Territories of the Pacific. The reason is not completely understood.[3] Occurrences such as these indicate there is some toxic effect or environmental factor. In reading about ALS, I have learned that there are links, in theory, between the disease and numerous other factors including viruses, exposure to various toxins or infectious agents, genetic factors, and immune system abnormalities, etc. When I think about the cause of Bill's illness, I consider the numerous times he has gone into burning factories and old houses. He must have breathed many toxic substances into his lungs. Protective masks were not required during the time he was a firefighter. I also wonder if there could be some sort of genetic factor involved in Bill's illness, but the family history does not support my concerns. His grandfather died of pneumonia at age forty-two, and of course, it is unknown whether he would have contracted the disease later in life. He fathered eight children, and seven lived to be old, but none was afflicted with ALS. Why motor neurons begin to die is a mystery, and future research may show that there are many contributing factors involved in the development of the disease.

Since there is little to offer in the form of medication for ALS, I have been searching the internet for any current or upcoming ALS clinical trials. In a clinical trial, drugs that could be effective in the treatment of the disease are often studied. I contacted an ALS clinic located in Florida earlier this week. There were several clinical trials pertaining to ALS posted on their website. Since my sister, Kathleen, and her family live in St. Augustine, I thought this clinic might be more convenient and easier for us to manage. The person on the phone told me she could place Bill on a waiting list for an evaluation to determine if he qualified for a clinical trial. She said the actual physician appointment for the evaluation could be as long as a year. Considering the often-rapid progression of the disease, I could not believe what she was telling me. My response to her was, "Never mind placing him on the waiting list—a year will be too late."

Friday, February 14, 2003

Bill saw the neurologist today, and the news was grim. Blood and urine tests to rule out other causes for his symptoms were negative, continuing to point to ALS as a diagnosis. The doctor described the two classifications of ALS: Sporadic ALS, and Familial ALS. He went on to say there are two types of Sporadic ALS. One type begins in the limbs, and the other type begins in the neck and chest. Since Bill has no family history of the disease, his diagnosis is Sporadic ALS with limb onset. The doctor explained in detail how the disease progresses. At first, there will be a gradual loss of use in the arms and legs. As the disease advances, he will eventually be unable to swallow, speak, or breathe. We learned that respiratory failure is usually the cause of death. It was an almost unbearable feeling to learn of all the assist devices Bill would need to become familiar with in the not too distant future. He would need a cane, walker, wheelchair, feeding tube, a computer device for communication, and finally a ventilator. A tracheotomy (an opening in the neck) would be necessary for ventilator use. The doctor stressed the fact that a ventilator would require around the clock care. He told Bill that he would recommend a feeding tube, but living on a permanent ventilator will have to be his own personal decision. Bill had no response to the statement.

The doctor cautioned Bill about the importance of choosing foods and liquids to avoid aspiration into the lungs. This could lead to serious aspiration pneumonia. He asked him to think about whether or not he would want CPR (cardiopulmonary resuscitation) in the event of a heart attack or other sudden occurrence. He requested a copy of Bill's Living Will, and he promised he would do everything possible to provide comfort as the disease progresses. He wrote a prescription for the drug Rilutek and said it was very expensive. Studies have shown that the drug extends life only three to six months. The doctor told Bill that he could decide if he wanted to take it. He did advise him to take Celebrex, a medication used to treat arthritis. Research has shown that the drug protects nerves in animal studies.

In the days preceding today's appointment, I encouraged Bill to ask for a second opinion regarding this life threatening disease. I have read that some patients have received an incorrect diagnosis. Even if the diagnosis is correct, there is a chance that another specialist may be more knowledgeable about the latest treatment and research. They might offer a more hopeful perspective. When I received my cancer diagnosis, I requested an evaluation by another oncologist. After the consultation, I felt relieved by the assurance that my treatment plan was standard practice. The fact that I had no lymph node involvement was a positive finding in the second doctor's evaluation, and I became more hopeful. Bill has been reluctant to ask for a second opinion because he believes it might offend his doctor. After much discussion, he finally concluded that the doctor's reaction to such a request was not an important issue. However, the office visit ended and he did not mention it to the doctor. Because of my need to have absolute confirmation in order to deal with this dreadful illness, I requested a referral for Bill to see another ALS specialist. On my request, the doctor willingly directed his office staff to arrange an appointment with the ALS specialist he had previously mentioned.

As the doctor closed the chart, he dictated a summary of Bill's illness and condition again in our presence. It did not seem possible that his words and this medical terminology could be related to this wounded person sitting beside me. There are really no words to describe the hopelessness and sadness of those moments. I held on tightly to Bill's hand as we listened once again to all the miserable details—while our world continues its downward spiral into disaster.

God Knows

God knows—not I—the devious way
Wherein my faltering feet may tread
Before, into the light of day,
My steps from out this gloom are led.
And since my Lord the path doth see,
What matter if 'tis hid from me?

His perfect plan I may not grasp,
Yet I can trust Love Infinite,
And with my feeble fingers clasp
The hand that leads me into light.
My soul upon His errands goes,
The end I know not…but God knows.

Author Unknown

God is our refuge and strength,
A very present help in trouble.

Therefore we will not fear,
Even though the earth be removed,
And though the mountains be
carried into the midst of the sea.

Psalm 46:1-2

Eight

Fear Filled Nights
Monday, February 24, 2003

Bill's choking episodes are occurring more frequently. This morning, he choked on cereal—yesterday it was chili. When he is choking, it is frightening because he panics, his face turns a bluish color, and he wheezes loudly until the choking episode subsides. Being a nurse trained in first aid techniques, I immediately prepare to perform the Heimlich maneuver or choking treatment. Each time, he puts out his hand to stop me. This is his way of letting me know it would not be necessary. Bill has had serious choking episodes before. The episodes usually occurred while he was eating meat. I have always attributed the choking to his tendency to eat too fast. One particular choking episode occurred just before we moved into our present home. He was sitting on the couch eating a piece of scorched pork chop. For some reason he has a taste for mildly burned food. On that particular day, he was unable to speak or breathe, and his face turned a deep purple color. I tried the Heimlich maneuver, but it was not working. We were frightened; nearing the panic stage. I had picked up the phone to call 911, but by that time he had been able to clear the obstruction from his throat. The choking episode was so severe that numerous small blood vessels ruptured in his face and neck causing him to have a bluish color for a couple of weeks. Ever since this upsetting experience, I have anxiety while Bill is eating. Recently, I have noticed he clears his throat frequently, and I am fearful this is the beginning of more serious swallowing problems.

    I have to keep busy in order to avoid thinking about the dreadful circumstances we are facing. Usually I occupy my time, as well as my mind, by cleaning the house or clearing out closets. This morning, I took our bedroom curtains down to wash them. While attempting to help me put the curtains back on the rods, Bill struggled to use fingers that would not follow directions. It was obvious that the disease is slowly but surely progressing just as the doctor predicted. I envision the point in time when he will be unable to walk, talk, or hold his grandchildren. When I think of him being totally paralyzed and bedridden, it is difficult beyond words to envision. On realizing that Bill may soon be disabled, I am preparing to have right total knee replacement surgery tomorrow (February 25). Two years ago, I had my left knee replaced due to the same condition of osteoarthritis. This surgery would have been necessary in the near future, but I am having it now because I must be physically capable to help Bill with a wide range of activities when the time comes. I will be in the hospital for several days, and I am already feeling worried and unsettled about leaving him alone. I have arranged for the neighbors to check on him; to make sure he is okay and has everything he needs.

    I cry often, especially at night, when thoughts of a grim future hinder my sleep. Trouble always seems to expand and press in when darkness comes. I know my own heartache is minimal when compared to Bill's personal anguish, so I do not cry in his presence. I believe he depends on me to stay strong and lead the way. I search for any words that may offer some measure of comfort, but usually I just say, "The Lord will help us with whatever we must face." When I pray, it is for great as well as small blessings. I pray Bill will be able to rest, sleep, and eat well enough to support his nutrition and weight. I pray the disease will advance slowly and allow him to have an acceptable quality of the life that remains. Most of all, I pray his suffering will not be great and that he will find peace for his soul. My prayers often end with, "Why Lord?"

Monday, April 7

It has been almost two weeks since my knee surgery. The surgery and recovery was much easier this time because I was more familiar with the process and knew what to expect. Nevertheless, surgery has brought about a temporary limitation in activity. It has still been a challenge to cope with the pain and comply with the aspects of postoperative therapy. I wanted to make thing easier for Bill, so I made plans before the surgery to remain in the hospital for physical rehabilitation an extra week. He was home by himself for longer than expected. I worried about him, but he has actually done quite well. He has had little difficulty with driving, and he visited me every day in the hospital. He is driving me to outpatient exercise sessions three days a week. As I write in my journal today, my recovery is going smoothly, and I have graduated from a walker to a cane.

Having another situation to deal with, to occupy our thoughts and time, has been good in many ways. Concentrating on my recovery is a welcome diversion. Unless something reminds us, he is unable to open a jar or pick up some small object; we forget for a time and continue daily life as usual. Bill is trying to help me with the cooking and other household chores. He prefers to mop the kitchen floor because I do not clean the corners to his satisfaction. This chore brings on difficult breathing, and he must stop and sit down at intervals to rest. He is still able to take care of his personal needs. In fact, unless you were with him all the time, you would not be able to recognize his limitations. At times, he tells me he has a feeling that he is being healed, but then he loses hope all over again. He is anxiously waiting to see the second ALS specialist on the fourteenth of this month. He believes this doctor will have an altogether different opinion.

Lately, we have not discussed the troubles and trials that lie ahead. Most of the time, unless the grandchildren are around, there is a quietness and sadness in the house. Bill goes to work; we go to church, and then out to eat on Sunday. Yet, there is no happiness or contentment in our lives, for this thing is never far from mind. The nights are becoming more difficult to manage. Even before my knee surgery, I often slept in another room because Bill had problems with sleep due to restlessness and leg cramps. Recently, he is up and down most of the night, and the sleeping medication provides little relief. Sometimes, in the middle of the night, his footsteps or the creaking of a door wakes me. He will climb into my bed, and he will be trembling all over. Once, he told me he was afraid of the disease and what it was doing to him. He spoke of it as if it were a living entity. Whenever I put my arms around him in order to comfort him, I can feel the muscle twitching and the bones beneath his thinning flesh. These are the most dreadful nights; filled with uneasiness and fear. As we huddle there in the darkness, it seems that morning will never come. Silent tears fill my eyes, and I wonder if it is possible to hate a disease.

Thursday, April 17, 2003

After I had recuperated for six weeks following knee surgery, we were able to travel to the out of state ALS clinic in order to keep Bill's appointment with the ALS specialist. He tolerated the trip well; if he became tired, he did not complain. Bill had to drive the long distance because I do not drive on the interstate highway. The numerous large trucks, which travel this curving highway over the mountains, make me extremely nervous. The neurologist here at home had highly recommended the doctor Bill was to see, and we were confident if there were any new knowledge or expertise available, it could be found here. Bill was hopeful, but I had a sense of doom—a feeling that we were facing another disappointing conclusion. The University affiliated hospital is approximately 265 miles from our home, and the hospital campus is very impressive. It is a large teaching hospital, and one of the nation's best academic medical centers. The broad range of services includes not only patient care, education, and community services, but research as well. When we at last found our way to the ALS clinic, the nurse clinician performed Bill's initial evaluation and completed the required paper-work. All the prior test results were available, so no additional tests or procedures were necessary.

Once the thorough physical examination and history was completed, the doctor did agree with the initial diagnosis of ALS. His manner was sympathetic and considerate as he answered our questions and presented the reasons for his opinion. He advised Bill to take the drug Rilutek in hopes of slowing the progression of the disease. He told us of an upcoming clinical trial and provided an opportunity for Bill to participate, and Bill agreed by stating, "If it will help someone who may one day find themselves in my shoes, I'll do whatever I can." In my opinion the most wonderful outcome, besides complete healing, would be disease remission. If the nerve destruction ceased, Bill would be able to adjust to the weakness the disease has already caused. Hope faded, however; when I asked the doctor about the chance for disease remission. He told me there have been some cases where disease progression has stopped or halted, but this is rare. Sometimes the disease progresses slowly, which allows some ALS patients to live up to fifteen years.

Our hearts were heavy with despair as we traveled back home that day. When you are clinging to hope, and hope is shattered, it is not easy to accept. I know Bill must have felt desolate and hopeless following the doctor's confirmation that he has ALS, but there is a wide gap between knowing and accepting. Being only human, we will continue to hold onto whatever optimism we can find. As long as there is a chance that the medication used in the course of the clinical trial, or the Rilutek, may be effective, hope will not be abandoned.

The first grandchild
Papaw and baby Justin
February 1992

*For the eyes of the Lord run to and fro
throughout the whole earth,
to show Himself strong on
behalf of those whose heart
is loyal to Him....*

2 Chronicles 16:9

Nine

Going Home
Monday, April 28, 2003

It is good to have a safe haven here on earth to run to when trouble comes to call. This place for me lies among the mountains where I spent the first seventeen years of my life. I can no longer visit my mother because she and my father died many years ago. My sister, Jean, my brother, Gary, and their families still live in the area. I went home today, and as Bill drove we traveled in near silence, immersed in our own thoughts. We have driven this road many times over the years, and the familiar country scenes of farms, fields, and wooded hills skipped by as I watched from the car window. As the low-lying, mist covered mountains came into view in the distance, I experienced an all too familiar feeling of belonging—of going home. There is an old saying, "Home is where we hang our memories." We may travel far and long from the place where memories began, but our heartstrings remain forever attached to home.

Erwin is a small town near the North Carolina border. It is nestled in a deep valley surrounded by the Appalachian Mountains. It is a quiet, serene place where everyone has knowledge of other people's business at any given time. I have always associated the area with stories my mother used to tell. One story concerned Mary the elephant. In the early 1900's, Erwin received notoriety for lynching a circus elephant from a one-hundred-ton railroad crane. It seems the elephant got angry and had crushed a circus worker to death in a nearby town. I suppose the hanging intended to punish Mary for her actions, but in my child's mind, I was sorry for the elephant who could not have known why they were punishing her. According to mama, they took Mary down from the crane, and the railroad yard became her grave. The elephant's bones still lie there today. When I tell people that Erwin is my hometown, some can recall hearing about this particular incident. Some books written about upper East Tennessee include this sad tale. As we drew nearer to the quiet, little town, other memories of the past flooded my thoughts.

I was born in the small community called Flag Pond, Tennessee. Over the years, if it became necessary to reveal my birthplace, people would often laughingly say something like, "What was that name again." The name Flag Pond actually has a unique origin. In the early 1800's, before the creeks in the area were rechanneled to build roads, several creeks converged to create swamps or ponds. Flag flowers or wild Irises grew in and around the ponds. Flag ponds are a natural habitat for waterfowl and some species of fish. You can find flag ponds in other places in the US, especially in Florida. When I was little, my maternal grandmother, Granny Moore, had a farm in Flag Pond. Our house was located just across the field from her house. My maternal grandfather was a county sheriff. In 1921, he was attempting to arrest a suspected criminal, and the man shot and killed him. My mother was twelve years old when her father died. Granny Moore was a strong-minded, independent woman of her time. She raised six children essentially on her own. She eventually lost her farm because of the inability to pay taxes on the land. These were the post-stock-market crash and depression years in the late 1920's and 1930's. I remember my grandmother giving food to needy people who stopped by her house. She would invite or allow the weary and wandering strangers to sleep in the barn and on her front porch.

My earliest memories were being at my grandmother's house or playing in the field that separated our two houses. While playing in a shallow creek with my little sister, Kathleen, and my older brother, Kenneth, Granny came and told us, "You have a little brother and sister." I was five years old when the twins, Jean and Jerry, were born. Gary, my youngest brother, came a few years later. My mother was thirty-six at the time, and I remember thinking she was too old to be having children. By the time I started school, we had moved to a house in the Temple Hill community. The rock house sat on approximately two acres of land. It had three bedrooms, a kitchen, a living room, a barn, and an outhouse. The house and land cost $800—unbelievable! Granny Moore lived in the house next door, and a large extended family of aunts, uncles, and cousins lived nearby. I could safely walk to school, houses of neighbors and relatives, and to church. There were no locked doors, no break-ins, and no attacks on children. It was a different world. The teachers taught grades one through eight in the three-room schoolhouse located just down the road. My third grade teacher was my all time favorite. Her students were required to salute the flag and recite the Lord's Prayer every day before class. Teachers used paddles in those days, and this teacher gave me my first and only paddling. The punishment was for biting the aggravating boy who sat in front of me. She also paddled the boy for pestering me.

Following the Great Depression, times were hard, and many people lived in poverty. Even in the years to follow, people would consider my family to be poor by today's standards. My father often did not have regular work, and he worked out of town much of the time. We had enough land to grow a vegetable garden, strawberries, and tobacco. We had a cow for milk and raised chickens and pigs for meat. My mother, Jessie, was short in stature but tall in spirit and determination. Like Granny Moore, she had the dubious task of raising six children with little help. She canned vegetables and fruit, and sewed most of the clothes the girls wore. She managed to keep us all in line with the help of a hickory switch. Looking back, I am sure there were many times when she felt defeated, disheartened, and overwhelmed, but she continued on—dependable and persistent. My mother and her mother, Granny Moore, were two of the strongest women I have ever known in my life. If I have any strength of character, it comes from the strong women in my family.

These mountains hold many memories—memories of trouble, unhappiness, sadness, and grief for loved ones who died. They also hold memories of happiness and joy, and a close extended family, church, and community. My best memories are of being with friends, playing in the woods, swimming in the creek, camping out at night, playing soft ball, hiking in the mountains, and trekking up the steep incline to the fire ranger station, which sat on top of the mountain. There was no TV so we listened to programs like "The Creaking

Door" on the radio, sang songs on the front porch with neighborhood kids, and told ghost stories that disturbed my dreams at night. My grandmother told an unforgettable story with the title, "The Icy Cold Fingers." In the scariest part of the story a woman's sister had died. That night as she slept with her arm relaxed over the side of her bed, icy cold fingers suddenly gripped her hand. To this day, my siblings and I are still leery of sleeping with our hands extended over the side of the bed. Some things remain forever imbedded in memory. I was nine years old when I accepted Christ as Savior in the little white church on the hill. Our dear, white-haired Baptist preacher baptized me in the creek that ran through the countryside in our community. I remember looking up to Heaven and talking with Jesus as a child. I sought His presence especially when I was frightened or worried about something. In spite of the difficulties and hard times, I have many wonderful and joyful memories of my childhood days growing up surrounded by those green, mist-covered mountains.

My interest in nursing began in high school Biology class. The complexities and intricate functions of the human body fascinated me. I wanted to learn more, but there was little money and a college education was not an option. After graduating high school and contemplating my future, I prayed that I might do something useful with my life. I soon enrolled in a nursing school located one-hundred miles from my home. I had a few homemade clothes, little money, but a lot of determination and faith. I learned of a government program that would pay my school tuition and expenses in return for a two-year commitment in the armed forces. I enlisted, with two of my classmates, in the Army Nurse Corp. We each received commissions as Second Lieutenants after graduation in 1957. The nurse corp. experience was a major blessing in my young life. I had the privilege of caring for young soldiers with life changing injuries, and I learned about true courage. In the years that followed, I had a nursing career that spanned forty-five years—the useful life I had prayed for. During those years, I witnessed much suffering, sadness, and death, and I learned that life is fragile. What lies ahead or what tomorrow holds is unknown to me, but I know who holds tomorrow, and He has said, "My grace is sufficient."

The rock house at Temple Hill near Erwin, Tennessee
My childhood home

He Giveth More Grace

He giveth more grace when the burdens grow greater,
He sendeth more strength when the labors increase;
To added affliction, He addeth His mercy;
To multiple trials, His multiplied peace.

When we have exhausted our store of endurance,
When our strength has failed ere the day is half done,
When we reach the end of our hoarded resources,
Our Father's full giving is only begun.

Fear not that thy need shall exceed His provision,
Our God ever yearns His resources to share;
Lean hard on the arms everlasting, availing;
The Father both thee and thy load will upbear.

His love has no limit; His grace has no measure.
His pow'r has no boundary known unto men;
For out of His infinite riches in Jesus,
He giveth, and giveth, and giveth again!

Annie Johnson Flint (1866-1932)

If any of you lacks wisdom,
he should ask God,
Who gives generously to all
without finding fault,
and it will be given to him.

James 1:5 (NIV)

Ten

A Clinical Trial
Sunday, May 18, 2003

On returning from the ALS clinic, Bill surprised me by saying he plans on requesting part-time work. He told me that he has tripped at least twice at work and almost fell. He will not admit it, but I believe the progressing muscle weakness is hindering him from climbing and moving around his work area in order to do his job. I think he is afraid his condition will worsen, or he will fall and sustain an injury while he is away from home. I am anxious about him being out of town in his condition, and I insist he has his cell phone handy at all times. Not going to work every day will be a huge change for Bill. While we were raising our two boys, he usually had part-time jobs on his days off from the fire hall. He did not mind hard work, and he usually worked with a fire fighter friend on various jobs. He was a plumber and house painter, and he helped one friend erect tall radio towers over the city. This caused me distress because of the extreme heights he was required to climb. He also worked with his best friend, Jim Woody, to renovate and rent old houses. His cutting back on work will be much safer for Bill and one less thing for me to fret and worry about.

Building and repairing things is something Bill does well, but he will no longer be able to enjoy this hobby. Over the years, he has painstakingly refinished several pieces of antique furniture. He was especially pleased to get a bargain on something. Once, he bought a cherry desk for $25 from an older couple while he was painting their house. On another job, a couple gave him a high-back oak bed and a cherry bed covered in pink paint. Removing the pink paint almost ended his fascination with restoring the old pieces. He later refinished an old oak mantle, my great grandfather's library table, his mother and grandmother's oak Singer sewing machines, and a couple of old trunks. He also built a grandmother clock from a kit. Our two sons used the antique beds until they left home. The oldest grandsons are making good use of them at present. I am thankful to have these items, which he restored with such great care. I hope they will serve to keep Bill's memory alive for the children and grandchildren.

When I reflect on the doctor's description of how ALS progresses and the loss in function Bill can expect, I feel frustrated that there is nothing to help him. There are no good drugs, no treatment; nothing to hang our hopes on. Prior to becoming aware of this, I had a small amount of optimism left, but it has been replaced by disappointment and doubt. There is only one drug available to treat one possible cause and that drug, Rilutek, approved for use in ALS by the Federal Drug Administration (FDA), increases survival only modestly. Bill is not sure that he should take the drug, but I feel he should take it if it can at least slow the disease. The deciding factor would be the quality of life during those additional months, and this is something we cannot predict. The doctor warned us that the medication was expensive, but nothing prepared me for the pharmacist's quote. A month's supply would cost $895. Bill is adamant when he says he is not going to take the drug unless insurance covers the cost. Since we have learned that the medical insurance he has through work will provide drug benefits and the co-pay will be minimal, he decided that he might as well go ahead and take the medication.

Bill sleeps very little and the pain in his knees and legs has worsened. The discomfort he describes is different from the cramping caused by the ALS. I suspect it is due to his arthritis because it is worse on walking and in certain lying positions. The doctor increased the pain medication, and I hope this drug will provide the pain relief and rest he needs. Despite the discomfort, he is determined to keep going—refusing to give in to his limitations. Keeping a nice yard has always been important, and this is the season for mowing, trimming, fertilizing, and all the other activities required for him to maintain a well-landscaped lawn. He will work in the yard all day until he becomes extremely fatigued. Sometimes, I think he pushes himself because the physical strength he has always relied on is slowly but surely betraying him. He seems to be testing his body to see how much it can tolerate. When I tell him to slow down and omit some of the yard work or hire someone to help, he pays no attention. Recently, he told me, "I'm not going to live much longer, and I intend to do as much as I can for as long as I am able."

Ever since we received the distressing news from the ALS clinic doctor, we have both been depressed and discouraged. There is much sadness and lack of peace in the house. Sometimes, I overhear Bill's phone conversations with family and friends. He verbalizes optimism that the new medication will work wonders, and he seems to have a lot of faith in the clinical trial. I wish I could be as hopeful. Bill has bouts of depression, but I seem to be in a constant state of gloominess. He told me it would help if I could be more positive and cheerful. How can I be cheerful when the future seems so bleak and hopeless? Despair visited me yesterday when I was alone in the house for several hours. Bill had gone out to eat then to a ballgame with friends. As I walked about the house and ate my evening meal alone, it occurred to me that this would be my life when he is no longer here. The reality brought deep sadness, and I began to weep. I have always been strong in trying times, but I do not know if I am strong enough to watch him die such a horrible death. I addition to the sadness, are the worrisome feelings of anger that wash over me time and time again. I am angry at this horrendous disease, angry because there is no treatment, and angry that my courage seems to have failed me. Sometimes I am angry at God and wonder if He has gone away, or does not care. Then I think He may be silent because my anger is drowning out his voice.

We both yearn to feel normal again, and to find some relief from this trying situation. If all goes as planned, we will visit my sister and her family in Saint Augustine, Florida, the last week in May. Bill likes to travel, but I am fearful the trip might be too much for him, but I do not discourage him from going. I want his quality of life to be the best it can be under the circumstances. On the way home from Florida, we plan to travel back to the ALS clinic. Bill has an appointment to undergo evaluation to determine if he qualifies for the upcoming clinical trial. I looked briefly into clinical trials when I received my breast cancer diagnosis. I have limited knowledge of the process, but

Bill depends on me to get the information, explain everything to him, and advise him on what he should do.

A clinical trial is a form of research study. Tests are carried out on people to see whether drugs, devices, treatments, or preventive measures are safe and effective for humans. In simple terms, patients participate to help doctors find better ways to improve health care treatment. The design, development, and process of a clinical trial is complicated and follows very strict guidelines and protocol. A clinical trial usually consists of two groups of participants, an experimental group and a control group. Group participants are typically chosen by chance or random draw, usually by computer assignment. The experimental group gets the treatment or drug in the study, and the control group gets the standard treatment for the illness or a placebo (sugar pill). The placebo will look like a medicine, but it is not a medicine. Clinical trials can be single or double blinded. In a single-blinded study, the patient does not know if they are in the experimental or control group. If the study is double-blinded, neither the clinician nor the patient knows which group is getting the experimental treatment. At the end of the study the outcomes, or sought for results (measurements that are defined at the outset of the trial) are compared and evaluated with the study results.[1]

Enrollment in a clinical trial is voluntary, but an evaluation and informed consent are required. Participants may have to be a certain age range, gender, stage of disease, and represent the disease as closely as possible. There is strict attention given to any anticipated risks for patients of a certain age, gender, race, physical condition, or for possible interaction with other drugs the person is taking. I understand that restrictions for ALS trial participants are often looser than for other conditions that are not so devastating or rapidly fatal.[1] Since Bill received his diagnoses in January, he is still in the early stages of the disease, and he already has several of the classical symptoms. ALS occurs most commonly between the ages of forty and seventy, but I am not sure if there are age requirements as related to the trial. I am encouraged that Bill stands a good chance to be chosen to participate. My primary concern is whether he will be able to complete and pass the pulmonary tests. I believe lung function has to be very near normal, or within strict perimeters of testing guidelines.

Bill's lung function could cause him to be excluded from the trial, and he will be devastated if he is unable to participate. All we can do is hope and pray for some good news for a change. If Bill does not meet the requirements, we will have to accept the inevitable and manage the illness the best way possible. In the meantime, my thoughts are with those who are anxiously awaiting the results of the random draw. No matter who is selected for the experimental group, my sincere hope is that the clinical trial will have a positive outcome; that answers will be revealed, which might help in the treatment of this dreadful disease.

Prayer

I asked for bread; God gave me a stone instead.
Yet while I pillowed there my weary head,
The angels made a ladder of my dreams,
Which upward to celestial mountains led.
And when I woke beneath the morning's beams,
Around my resting place fresh manna lay;
And praising God, I went upon my way
For I was fed.

God answers prayer; sometimes, when hearts are weak,
He gives the very gifts believers seek.
But often faith must learn a deeper rest
And trust God's silence when he does not speak.
For He whose name is Love will send the best.
Stars may burn out, nor mountain walls endure,
But God is true. His promises are sure
For those who seek.

Author unknown

Even to your old age, I am He,
And even to gray hairs I will carry you!
I have made, and I will bear;
Even I will carry, and will deliver you.

Isaiah 46:4

Eleven

Longing for a Miracle
Wednesday, June 6, 2003

The devilish side of Bill's personality can be endearing yet problematic at times. Living at the fire hall for half his life, he has had many opportunities to become an expert at being a prankster. Pulling pranks and tomfoolery on each other was one way used by the firefighters to pass the time between alarms. Bill never means any harm, but he relishes catching people off guard in order to pull a trick or a joke. Sometimes his endeavors to be funny get him into trouble. I remember one particular incident, which occurred while we were standing in line with my brother, Jerry, and his family to tour the White House. Bill had made some sort of witty remark about whoever happened to be the US President at the time. I do not recall the exact words he used, but they must have been significant enough to cause alarm and elicit a response. Almost immediately, the security police appeared. I suppose there were listening devices planted along the walkway. They pulled Bill out of line and took him away for questioning. They released him a short time later after he convinced his captors that he was only joking. I was furious with him because the experience was frightening as well as embarrassing. Nevertheless, incidents such as this have not deterred him from his devilish deeds. He especially delights in "getting the best" of family and close friends who know him well. During our stay in Florida; however, I noticed that he was quiet and subdued much of the time. It was obvious he had to make a concerted effort to be his usual jovial, good-humored self. I feel sad because this change in his personality causes me to better understand his state of mind and admit that this disease has already begun to steal the joy from his life. I only hope his gloominess is temporary, because his sense of humor will help him navigate the grim and humorless times that are sure to come.

We always look forward to going to Saint Augustine to visit Kathleen, Manuel, and their daughter, Cynthia, but this time it was with a good amount of trepidation. Considering all Bill has to contend with, the leg cramps, weakness, sleepless nights, and the depression, I was concerned the trip would be too wearisome and unpleasant—too much for him to handle. I dreaded the almost six-hundred-mile trip because Bill had to do all the driving. I do not assist in driving on the interstate highways because I get too nervous. He obviously sensed my concern about his welfare, for along the way he would attempt to reassure me by telling me every now and then, "I'm doing just fine." Traveling the rather long distance to Saint Augustine in one day was tiring, but Bill tolerated it well. I have never enjoyed traveling a long distance by car. I am uncomfortable much of the time due to stiff, painful, and restless legs, so we stopped several times along the way. During our stay in Florida, Bill continued to have leg cramps especially at night. He was quite miserable until the pain medication took effect. One day, we went to Fort Myers to visit friends, Jim and Barbara Woody. They have a boat docked in one of the waterways, and they live on the boat most of the summer months. While we were in Florida, our sons notified us that our house and Bill's truck had received damage from an unusual tornado-like hailstorm, which had passed through our neighborhood. They provided internet images of Bill's severely dented truck, the damaged house, and the amazing piles of large hail covering the lawn and back deck.

We left Saint Augustine and traveled to Columbia, SC, to visit my brother, Jerry, who is retired from his job as a railroad train master. Jerry lives alone in his condo with his animals. He rescues abandoned dogs and cats from the surrounding fields and woods. He takes them to a veterinarian and cares for them until they are well enough to go to a no-kill animal shelter for adoption. He usually has five or six dogs and as many as twenty cats on his property. It devastates him if one of his animals gets sick. If the animal dies, he has the body cremated and keeps the ashes. His little bird had recently died, and he showed us the small urn which sits on his mantle. Jerry has a compassionate heart for all animals. Recently, he started feeding pigeons that roost near his house. Now, every time the birds see his red SUV pull into the parking lot, they gather around in droves waiting for their bird food to be scattered. Following our visit with Jerry, we drove to the ALS clinic for Bill's appointment relating to the clinical trial. During the visit, he had many tests. One test, a Pulmonary Function Test (PFT), measures lung function. A Forced Vital Capacity (FVC) is an important component of the PFT. It measures the amount of air that can be expelled from the lungs in one forced breath.[1] Bill's FVC was

78 percent, which is lower than normal. This particular information was distressing, and I viewed it as an ominous sign. It indicates that the nerve destroying disease has already affected the diaphragm, the abdominal muscle that is important for the exhalation of air and the function of breathing.

On the way home, Bill surprised me by saying, "I've decided to quit my job." He said he has lost interest in work; that he needs to catch up on things needing done around the house. The decision must have been a difficult one, but I am glad he is quitting. It will be a welcome relief not to agonize when he is away from home. I am sure he desires to make the best of the time he has left of his life, and work is not a priority. Later, he verbalized concern about our finances and asked if we could manage if he stopped working. I assured him we would be fine. My main concern at present is making plans to return to the ALS clinic in two weeks for the results of the clinical trial testing. I am trying not to place too much hope in this undertaking, but if he does not qualify for the trial, earthly hope is all but lost.

After our return home, we had to contend with the damage from the hailstorm. Two large windows in the kitchen on the front of the house were shattered, and Bill's truck had broken windows and large dents throughout. The roof had sustained damage in several places and there were several holes in the stucco on the house. Bill has been busy obtaining estimates, checking insurance, and arranging for all the necessary repairs. The roof needs replacing, and estimates to repair the truck are already at $6000. He is mostly distressed over the damage to his truck. Nevertheless, the activity is helping to keep his mind off his illness—for this, I am thankful.

June 18, 2003

During the second trip to the ALS clinic, we learned of Bill's acceptance to participate in the clinical trial, and he was elated. It is to be a double-blinded study for the drug Celebrex. He is already taking an average dose of the drug prescribed by his neurologist. The trial dose of the Celebrex is four times the average dose. Three-hundred people in twenty-five medical centers across the US will participate in the trial. Some people will receive the placebo or sugar pill and others the Celebrex. Twice as many people are to receive the Celebrex than will receive the placebo. The clinical trial is to last one year.[2] Bill will be required to return to the clinic every three to four weeks. During these visits, there will be a close evaluation of his muscle strength, breathing strength, activity of daily living functions, and any side effects related to the medication. Before we left the clinic, the nurse gave Bill a supply of capsules and dosing instructions. She cautioned that we must keep extremely careful records of the doses. We will not know if he is the experimental group or the control group until the study ends and the results are calculated.

There will soon come a time when Bill will not be physically able to drive the long distance to the ALS clinic, and it will present a transportation problem. I will need to think about family or friends who may be available to drive him to his clinic appointments. I feel that Bill's acceptance to participate in the clinical trial is a blessing and an answer to prayer. For now, I will have faith and believe that the Lord knows our needs, and He will make a way.

Answers to Prayer

Answers to prayer come in various ways,
Sometimes in minutes, sometimes in days.
Some may take years to freely unfold
The harvest of love and blessings they hold.

Answers to prayer come in various forms,
Sometimes in sunlight; sometimes in storm.
Some blossom early; some blossom late,
But each one will flower, have faith and wait

        Author unknown

Standing in line at the White House
Shirley R, Nicole, Jerry, Bill and Shirley K.

Bill, Shirley, Kathleen and Manuel
Mt. Snow, Vermont

*And we know that all things
work together for good
to those who love God,
to those who are called
according to His purpose.*

Romans 8:28

Twelve

All Things for Good
Monday, June 30, 2003

Trouble sometimes comes in clusters or layers, with one layer complicating the one that follows. A dilemma has arisen regarding knee replacement surgery for Bill. He can barely walk due to the pain in both knees. The diagnosis is severe osteoarthritis, but the cortisone injections he had last week helped very little. He would be a high surgery risk because of his poor lung function, and the postoperative therapy would be very hard on him. My concerns are primarily for pain relief, but I also want him to be able to walk for as long as the disease allows. I did not have to worry long because Bill made his own decision by telling me, "Why should I have surgery for bad knees when I'm going to lose the use of my legs?" It occurred to me that if he is receiving the actual Celebrex in the clinical trial, the larger dose might work to relieve the arthritic knee pain. In the meantime, he continues to do the yard work and is able to mow using the riding lawn mower. The lawn care takes him much longer than usual because the smallest amount of exertion brings on shortness of breath. Each day, we wait and hope that this nightmare could eventually have an end.

Sunday, July 6, 2003

A dear friend and fellow firefighter, Buster Watson, drove Bill to the ALS clinic this week. He was to have a spinal tap and could not drive afterward. With a spinal tap (lumbar puncture), the doctor inserts a special needle into the lower back and into the spinal canal (the area around the spinal cord). The pressure in the spinal canal and brain is then measured, and a small amount of cerebral spinal fluid (CSF) goes to the laboratory for analysis. I have not yet learned the significance of the spinal tap as it relates to the clinical trial, but it is painfully obvious that Bill's illness is progressing. Before church on Sunday, he was unable to button his shirt and pants because of the weakness in his fingers. He struggled for a while, but then he reluctantly asked for my help. I have noticed he holds eating utensils differently, having to use more fingers to hold his fork or knife. He is beginning to have difficulty cutting his food. I hesitate to help him because I know how much he relishes his independence. However, there is some light in the darkness. Maybe it is only wishful thinking, but since he has been taking the drug Rilutek, he seems to have less difficulty swallowing, and the choking episodes have decreased in frequency.

Monday, July 21, 2003

For several months, Bill and I have been visiting a Baptist church in our neighborhood because Bill very much enjoys the pastor's sermons. A recent Sunday message caused Bill to worry that his illness could be punishment for sin. After the service, he was quiet and withdrawn. It was obvious that he was troubled about something. On questioning he said, "I'm just having a bad period." This is his way of letting me know he is depressed or worried. He went on to say, "If God is not punishing me, why has He not answered my prayers or the prayers of others on my behalf?" I cannot know the depths of Bill's despair, and any words that come from my mouth will not be sufficient for comfort and reassurance. I must always depend on the Lord to put the right words on my tongue. I reminded him there are many reasons for trials, and that Christ has already paid the price for sin—only repentance is required. I did not know what else to say except that I know for certain that God loves us and will provide for our needs. The conversation ended with Bill's declaration, "It will have to be worked out between me and God."

We made a decision to join the church we have been visiting. Last Sunday, we went forward as is customary when the pastor gave the invitation to accept new members. We discovered we must attend classes for membership consideration. If accepted, we would be required to serve in a church ministry. I was concerned because I feared that the ministry activities would be beyond Bill's physical capabilities, so we decided to postpone our request for membership. We are not familiar with this particular rule and practice in a Baptist church, but we continue to attend services there. Bill seemed disappointed and discouraged. Perhaps he believes that joining a church is a step closer to making things right with God. In our quest for further spiritual support and reassurance, we often watch religious programs on TV. One televangelist recently recited meaningful scripture from the Apostle Paul's writings in the book of Romans.

> *"And we know that all things work together for good to those who love God, to those who are called according to His purpose."*
>
> Romans 8:28

The heart of the message was that "all things" include suffering. Sometimes there is no other way, except through suffering, to bring us to complete dependence on God. The resulting good, which comes from our trials, is according to His purpose and as seen from His prospective. He went on to say that nothing takes God by surprise, and tragedy does not occur because He was not watching. When sorrow and misfortune touches us, God is there to make something worthwhile out of the pain we bear. The message ended with this statement, "The crucifixion of Christ was the vilest and most evil act ever committed by man, but it resulted in the greatest good."

It all makes sense when viewed from a biblical prospective, but it would be wonderful if we could only view our present circumstances through the eyes of God. It is difficult to comprehend, especially in the midst of suffering that He is at work; that anything good could result from a tragedy such as this. However, we are told in the Bible that everything will be made clear in the hereafter, *"For now we see in a mirror dimly, but then face to face...."*(*1 Corinthians 13:12*). Until then, we have no choice but to accept what God has allowed and trust in His wisdom, that He has a better plan—a greater purpose. We both hope and pray that our children and grandchildren will learn from Bill's struggle, and will not fail to recognize the need for Christ's presence in their lives.

Even as Christians, we have less need for God when life is going smoothly and trouble has not reared its ugly head. We lose ourselves in everyday life and drift away from things that matter. When trouble and trials come, God is usually the first to receive the blame and responsibility as we cry out to Him in our anguish. Nevertheless, He has patience and does not fail to hear our cries for help and penitence.

"The Lord is not slack concerning His promise…, but is long suffering toward us, not willing that any should perish, but that all should come to repentance." (2 Peter 3:9)

I have regret due to the fact that Bill and I had become complacent and neglectful of our own Christian faith over the past several years. We left the church we had attended since our children were small. It seems the pastor had fallen from grace in the eyes of the congregation, and we became disappointed and disillusioned. I had to work my share of weekends because hospitals never close, and Bill had to work many weekends with his job as a firefighter, so we did not attend church regularly. Since we moved to our present home, we have visited several Baptist churches in our community, but have previously been unable to decide on a church home.

When I received my breast cancer diagnosis, I realized that sometimes God gives us trials, or increases the weight of our burdens, to remind us how much we need His mercy and grace; to get us back on the right track. Each day, as I watch Bill struggle to come to terms with his illness, it is obvious he has a great need to reconcile his faith and restore his relationship with Christ. During one discussion, he told me, "Maybe I'm not deserving of God's grace." I attempted to remind him that we never deserve God's grace—it is freely given; that forgiveness and restoration are always God's way. Every time I see him sitting quietly in his recliner reading his Bible, I am encouraged and hopeful that he will somehow find the assurance and peace for his soul that he so desperately desires.

Wednesday, July 30, 2003

Our son, John, drove his dad to the ALS clinic this week for his follow-up appointment related to the clinical trial. If Bill is receiving the actual experimental drug, he seems to be tolerating it well. His knee pain is much better, and he is able to walk with little discomfort. On one occasion and without Bill's knowledge, I compared the taste of the experimental drug with the contents of an actual Celebrex capsule, and they had a similar taste. Because of this, and especially due to the knee pain relief, I am encouraged that he is receiving the real Celebrex in the clinical trial. God is still at work.

As long as I have known Bill, he has expressed a desire to tour the western states. He was in the National Guard for several years, and he once attended a training session for two weeks in Arizona. He loved the ruggedness and beauty of the wide-open spaces. One day I suggested that he think about going out West before the summer ends. I wanted him to go before the disease robbed him of more function, and I recommended that he discuss it with his friend, Jim Woody. They could fly to a central state, rent a car, and then travel to whatever state they want to visit. He hesitated at first, because he felt that we could not afford the cost of such a trip. However, he contemplated the idea and decided that he wanted to pursue it, and he lost little time before discussing the idea with Jim. I do not know if Jim could take the time from his busy schedule, or if he even had a desire to go out West, but he readily agreed that they should plan the trip. Knowing Jim as I do, he would do anything to help Bill during this difficult time in his life. When Buster Watson heard about the trip, he was anxious to be included. They have decided to travel in Bill's truck. Before long, another friend, Bill Warwick, became the fourth firefighter to be taking the Western tour.

For several weeks, the four firefighters have been involved in the process of making trip plans. They have been gathering maps and compiling information about what routes they will take, and especially the interesting places they would like to visit. Bill and I have been busy packing his things and trying to anticipate any special needs he might have. Since he has problems managing buttons, we packed slipover shirts. I suggested pants with elastic in the waist, but he prefers to wear his jeans. He said, "The guys will help me with the buttons." He is able to pull on his socks with some difficulty, but his shoes are slip-on with no ties. He seems happier and more content than he has been in months. He has even been able to smile and laugh now and then. I am glad that he has something besides this dreadful illness to look forward to—to occupy his heart and mind. I am thankful that he will be able to fulfill a lifelong dream; a dream that has now become a dying wish.

For he shall give His angels charge over you
To keep you in all your ways.

In their hands they shall bear you up.
Least you dash your foot
against a stone.

Psalm 91:11-12

Thirteen

A Wish Fulfilled
Friday, August 1, 2003

Following several weeks of meticulous preparation, the four fighters left today for their western adventure. They had an SUV full of luggage, bags of snacks to munch on, and hearts full of joyous anticipation. Due to a plan change, they set out in Bill Warwick's GMC Yukon. On the back of the vehicle, they had mounted a large red and white sign announcing, "Four Retired Firefighters from Knoxville, Tennessee Traveling the US." They were like excited little boys as they lined up behind the SUV for me to take a group photo. I am so thankful Bill is able to go on this trip, and I believe he will be fine. He will be able to shower, dress himself, and shave with his electric razor. He will need some assistance cutting his food, and he will not be able to walk very fast and will require rest periods. The other men are aware of his limitations, and I know they will help him with whatever he needs. They are big men, and they would probably carry him if it became necessary. They will not expect him to help with the driving, so he can just sit back and enjoy the view. Before they drove away, I kissed Bill goodbye, and I asked the Lord to watch over and protect him. I thanked Him for these three men and their beautiful gesture of friendship. I am so very appreciative that Jim, Buster, and the other Bill recognized my sense of urgency for taking the trip before his illness destroys all possibility. I will be grateful beyond forever. I am especially thankful that Bill is free of pain. "All things work together for good."

Saturday, August 9, 2003

Since Bill left, I am trying to reconcile to being alone in the house for a few weeks. The western trip is to last approximately one month. We have never been apart this long before, and a feeling of loneliness comes quickly. As the days go by, I have been getting almost daily reports from all points west. Bill has said more than once, "I'm having a great time." The first week they traveled through eight states. In Missouri, they met a big-rig truck driver who offered them a free week vacation in his condominium, which was located in Corpus Christy, Texas. They visited an Amish farm in Iowa where they bought jalapeno cheese, sweet rolls, and candy onion. They watched an Indian Paw Wow in Ottumwa, Iowa. They visited the Hormel plant in Freemont, Nebraska, the only place in the world that makes Spam. The Nebraska State Police pulled them over for speeding on Highway 275. The officer gave them a warning ticket.

One of the highlights of this first week was a visit to Mount Rushmore near Rapid City, South Dakota. In Sturgis, South Dakota, they encountered a Harley Davidson motorcycle convention with over a million people attending. They passed through a town in Wyoming called Van Tassle that listed a population of 18. While touring the Grand Teton National Park located near Jackson Hole, Wyoming, they saw the Snake River and the cloud layered, snow covered Teton Mountains. They had to wait to see the Old Faithful Geyser blow in Yellowstone National Park. Bill told me they had traveled across the Continental Divide twice in the same day. So far, he seems to be tolerating the trip well. By the end of the first week, they had arrived in Butte, Montana. They had driven 3,048 miles.

I talk with Bill by phone every day. He told me about seeing a wide variety of animals including bear, elk and deer, mountain goat, coyote, moose, eagle, buffalo, and large herds of antelope. They are currently traveling through landscape where much is semi-desert, sagebrush dotted, rugged and grand in size. It is much different in contrast to our green, mist-covered mountains here at home. Bill describes the expansive scenery as, "amazing and breathtaking." With excitement in his voice, he repeatedly says, "I love it all."

Evidently, the firefighter sign on the back of the SUV has drawn a lot of positive attention. They have met and had conversations with other firefighters along the way, and they have had handshakes and pats on the back in places where they have stopped. They are receiving many waves and honking of horns from other travelers on the road. Everyone knows that firefighters enjoy food, and it appears they are carefully seeking out the best places to eat. Some of the places they have eaten include Cowboys, White Buffalo Café, and Whiskey Creek Steak House. They all like breakfast food, and the goal is to find the place that serves the best biscuits and gravy. According to Bill's latest report, "Cowboys is the winner."

Thursday, August 14, 2003

I am attempting to keep busy in order to avoid thinking about what the future holds. I am working a few days at the hospital, and do not rush to come home to an empty house. I have gone out to lunch with friends a few times, and babysitting little Andrew is a welcome diversion—he keeps me busy. Yesterday, I cleaned the house and rearranged closets, but nothing really eases my trepidation. The nights are the most difficult. After our sons were gone from home and Bill was at the fire station for twenty-four hour shifts, I was not afraid to be alone at night. There was only an occasional sense of uneasiness. In his absence currently, I have an increased sense of apprehension. I must make sure doors are locked, the alarm system set, and the phone numbers of neighbors are close by my bedside.

Last Sunday, I attended a family reunion with our sons and their family. The reunion was a celebration for relatives of Bill's mother. We were able to renew acquaintances with people we had not seen in years. We had a delicious meal, looked at family photos and the old family bible, sang songs, and took group pictures. Everyone had a great time. Our three-year-old Andrew volunteered to perform and delighted everyone by singing a song called, "Herman the Worm." When I am not working or keeping Andrew, I continue searching the internet for any new or updated information regarding ALS. I was shocked to learn that the cost of care can reach as much as $200,000 a year. I assume this would be for someone who is ventilator dependent requiring around the clock care. I decided to keep records of all costs related to Bill's care. At times, the reality of where our life may be heading hits me. Bill will return from this trip, but I visualize a future when he no longer comes home. When that time comes, I pray that I will never engage in dwelling on loneliness and self-pity.

Monday, August 18, 2003

The retired firefighters have covered a lot of ground over the past ten days. They traveled to Glacier Park located in northwest Montana and drove along the "Going to the Sun Road," which trails the park's two largest lakes. They ate the "best ever" pie and razzleberry ice cream at a place called The Park Café. They traveled through Idaho toward Washington State passing hundreds of miles of humongous fields of wheat. Bill laughed when he told me, "Guess what, we won two dollars in the Washington State lottery." A man, at the Husky's Market in Moro, Oregon, gave them two large bags of potato chips to munch on along the way. Driving down USA Highway 95, they could see the snow capped Mount Jefferson in the distance. The beauty of the volcanic Crater Lake in Crater Lake, Oregon, awed them. The collapse of an ancient volcano formed the lake millions of years ago.

At Mother's Café in Klamath Falls, Oregon, they played the game of Keno, but there were no big winners. Entering California, they saw snow covered Mount Shasta located in the northern corner of the state. They spent a rest-day in Reno, Nevada, and visited the Silver Dollar Saloon in Virginia City where Bill Knight won a bottle of Champagne.

They were in Lake Tahoe, Nevada, when news was received that a friend and fellow firefighter had died back home in Knoxville. They traveled the 300-mile long USA Highway 50, known as the loneliest highway in America. They met a group of local firefighters in Beaver, Utah, and gave them Knoxville, Tennessee, firefighter caps. After traveling through Kenab, Utah, they entered the Grand Canyon National Park where they viewed the canyon from the north rim. The visit to Pike's Peak near Colorado Springs, Colorado, proved to be a challenge. The high mountain altitude caused them to have difficulty breathing. Today, on my birthday, they visited the Murrah Building Monument in Oklahoma City, Oklahoma. It brought back memories of the 1995 Murrah Building bombing, which killed one-hundred-sixty-eight people. Bill described a large statue of Jesus weeping, which touched his heart. He said, "It was the saddest place."

Wednesday, August 20, 2003

As I write this journal entry, the four retired firefighters have completed their tour of the West. The trip lasted nineteen days, with a total of 7,775 miles across sixteen states. They returned home yesterday afternoon. They were hot and tired but still elated by all they had seen and done. The trip was not as long as originally planned, which was probably a good thing. Bill brought gifts of western jewelry for the girls in the family and tee shirts for all the guys. He brought me a jacket from Zion Canyon, Utah, for my birthday. Buster kept a detailed account of the trip in his personal journal. They took a photo of the weeping Jesus as well as a ton of other photos in order to preserve those special memories. Bill Warwick commented in Buster's journal that several people had asked him how four men, in such close quarters, got along so well on such a hard trip. He said they had already learned to live together during long hours at the fire station, and they were like family. The main reason was because they all shared a Christian faith and fellowship.

Three great friends
Crater Lake, Oregon
August 10, 2003
Bill Warwick, Jim Woody, and Buster Watson

Friends are angels who lift our feet

and bear us up,

when our own wings are broken,

and we cannot fly.

Is there no other way-Oh God,
Except through sorrow, pain, and loss
To stamp Christ's likeness on my soul,
No other way except the cross.

And then a voice stills all my soul,
That stilled the waves of Galilee.
Cans't thou not bear the furnace,
If midst the flames, I walk with thee.

I bore the cross, I know its weight.
I drank the cup I hold for thee.
Cans't thou not follow where I lead,
I'll give thee strength-Lean hard on Me.

Author unknown

Jesus wept. John 11:35

Four retired firefighters from
Knoxville, Tennessee, touring the USA
August 1, 2003

At the top of Pikes Peak near Colorado Springs, Colorado
August 2003

Be anxious for nothing, but in everything
by prayer and supplication,
with thanksgiving,
Let your requests be known to God;

And the peace of God,
which surpasses all understanding,
will guard your hearts and minds
through Christ Jesus.

Philippians 4:6-7

Fourteen

Loss and Helplessness
Monday, September 1, 2003

Bill seemed proud to report that he had but one choking episode while he was away. The incident occurred while he was eating a piece of candy. He said the guys had to pull the SUV off the highway, remove him from the car, and administer first aid until he was able to recover. These three men were emergency first responders before they retired as firefighters, so he was in safe hands. He had not informed me beforehand, but when he stepped out of the SUV on his return home that day, a bandage was covering a cut over his right eye. He said he tripped and fell over a gas pump hose at a filling station—it was an accident. It is more likely that his weakened leg muscles prevented him from picking up his feet while walking. In the days following his return home, Bill seemed fatigued and listless. He said the trip was hard at times because they traveled an average of 600 miles a day. The trip was cut short because one of the guys had pressing business to take care of at home. Nevertheless, he had enjoyed the trip so much; he would have stayed an entire month if possible. He casually mentioned that he might want me to scatter his ashes over the Glacier Lake area in Montana. He said it was the most beautiful place they visited—his favorite spot.

Bill is gradually recovering from the trip euphoria as daily life presents itself. However, there is disappointing evidence of further disease progression in just these few weeks. It is obvious he has lost more weight. He admitted to having a poor appetite the entire time he was away, and he attributes this to the numerous medications he is required to take. His voice appears weaker, his speech is more slurred, and it has a coarse, raspy sound. He told me about increased weakness in his legs, especially if he had to walk a lot or was required to climb more than a few steps. The lagging behind bothered him because the guys had to stop and wait for him to catch up. Another problem occurred while at the top of Pike's Peak. He became so short of breath, dizzy, and weak; he had to be given oxygen and be brought back down to a lower altitude. Evidently, Jim, Buster, and Bill Warwick had taken very good care of him. He said, "They treated me like a baby." Before Bill left on his trip, I had given him a journal for recording each day's occurrence. Later, when I opened the book to read what he had written, I noticed that he had scribbled only a few almost illegible lines on the first few pages. His excuse was, "I began having trouble holding the pencil, so I just gave up."

Other people have begun to notice the change in Bill's voice. They often ask him to repeat what he says because of the slurred speech, and this is obviously very frustrating for him. He is no longer able to sing in church, something he has always enjoyed. His voice will be almost normal in the morning, but it becomes weaker and more slurred as the day advances. His walk has slowed, and he does not pick his feet up normally causing occasional stumbling. The worsening breathing problems are beginning to limit daily activities, and there is a decline in his overall strength. Recently, because his arms are so weak, he was unable to lift little Andrew, who weighs 35 pounds, onto the low branch of a tree. The increased twitching in his arms and chest indicate increased nerve destruction. He has become so accustomed to the twitching, that most of the time, he is not aware it is happening.

Even with medication, Bill sleeps but a few hours at night, so he is tired and irritable during the day. He is sad, bored, and frustrated due to limited activity. His current distress is heartbreaking, and I can only anticipate a worsening of the situation. He is unable to gain weight in spite of drinking milkshakes and other high caloric dietary supplements. During the last visit to his primary physician, the doctor instructed him to stop the cholesterol lowering medication he had been taking for several years. He did not give a reason for stopping the drug, but I could understand and agree. I could imagine that Bill was interpreting the doctor's thoughts to be, "There is no need to be concerned about elevated cholesterol in a dying patient." I am thankful there is one less pill for him to swallow, but I am also saddened because of the despair and hopelessness he must be feeling.

Saturday, September 13, 2003

Bill made plans to do the fall yard maintenance this week. He went to the store to buy fertilizer, but he was unable to lift the fertilizer bags onto the back of his truck. He reluctantly had to ask the store personnel for help. Del Robeson, our good next-door neighbor, helped him to unload the bags and spread the fertilizer over the yard. A few days later, he discovered that the windows on the outside of our house needed minor repairs, but when he began the work he found he could not open and close them by himself. He was determined, however, and with my help and some difficulty, he was able to hold the brush well enough to apply paint to the window casings. He can operate the riding mower, but using other items of yard equipment to trim shrubs and cut weeds is becoming a difficult process. Recently, I notice he is having problems turning the ignition key on his truck. Once, he had to ask me to come outside and turn the water faucet off because he was unable to turn the knob. Sometimes, when these incidents occur, he will become very frustrated and angry. He occasionally uses colorful language to express his frustration. As the disease progresses, I am becoming more concerned about leaving him alone while I am at work, and I probably call too often to check on him. My heart breaks as I witness his attempts to cope with the increasing functional losses. I remain amazed that he is still able to joke and find occasional humor in such a dreadful situation.

On a recent Friday night, we went with two other couples to John and Pat Holland's home for dinner. The men were long-time friends of Bill and John. It was an enjoyable evening with a great meal and much reminiscing about bygone days. Bill was having more difficulty swallowing, and I hoped he would be able to manage his food without choking. During the meal, I noticed he ate slower than usual, took smaller portions of food, and drank liquid more often. He got through the meal without incident, but watching his efforts was heartbreaking. He can still cut most of his food, but he cannot tear open pre-packaged items such as salt, pepper, and ketchup. Because of the difficulty in swallowing, I am exploring ways to alter foods he likes in order to provide a consistency that will be easier to swallow. Being a country boy Bill is fond of corn bread, but when he eats it, it usually brings on a choking episode. I have found he tolerates spoon bread very well. I make the spoon bread with less corn meal and more flour, eggs, and milk. He also likes peanut butter and crackers. I dread the sad day when he can no longer enjoy his favorite foods and snacks.

Friday, September 26, 2003

It has been nine months since Bill received the ALS diagnosis. The changes in his physical function are painful to watch, but I am learning to be thankful for the blessings that belong to each day. I am thankful that I can understand his speech; that he is able to swallow, to walk, and do most of the things he needs to do. I am thankful that I am able to get up every day and have the strength to help Bill with whatever he needs on any particular day. I am exceedingly thankful for our family.

The grandchildren are curious and beginning to be aware that there is something wrong with their Papaw, and they are asking questions. The nine-year-old boy, John Morgan, overheard a request for prayer for Bill at his church one Sunday. Since that time, if John Morgan finds out that Bill has been to see a doctor he wants to know what the doctor said. We have attempted to explain Papaw's illness in terms the children can understand, but it is complicated and difficult. John Morgan asked his Papaw one day if he was going to die. It was obvious that Bill was searching for the right words to say—trying hard not to upset this sensitive young boy. After a long pause, he finally said, "I am going to die, but not for a long time."

The guys have gathered several times at our house over the past several weeks to talk and look over their photos. It is heart warming to hear them laughing and talking as they happily relive their western excursion. Bill Warwick put together Buster's carefully recorded account of each day's location and events in a binder; with a copy for each firefighter. The beauty and grandeur of the landscape, mountains, and lakes they had captured on film are truly amazing. As always, I was in awe by the greatness of the One who created it all. As I thumbed through the large volume of photographs, I came across photos of the weeping Jesus statue that Bill had so tenderly described. All the beautiful photographs remind me that God keeps unbroken vigilance over all of His creation. But most of the time, the work of His hands goes unnoticed as we concentrate on living life; seldom looking up—taking all of His love and care for granted.

Because of the love and sacrifice of three comrade firefighters and devoted friends, Bill was able to experience a wonderful adventure, and I will be grateful beyond forever. In addition to Bill being given the strength to endure the tour and the pleasure it provided, I believe this trip served a special and greater purpose. Maybe the Lord wanted to remind him of His power and presence. Perhaps, He only desired to instill His peace in a hurting heart that knows only loss, hopelessness, and fear.

...

Great are the Works of His Hands

There's none but our God who can fashion
A marvelous world so fair,
For He hold the key to creation,
In earth, sky, and sea, and air;
From each glorious snow capped mountain,
To each tiny grain of sand,
From the oceans to sparkling fountains,
Great are the works of His hands!

There's none like our Heavenly Father
Whose love mortals cannot explain,
Who tenderly watches each sparrow
And healeth the crushed hearts of men.
From each song that springs within me,
To angels' fair song in that land,
There's one that shall echo eternally,
Great are the works of His hands.

Author unknown

Justin and Papaw, December 1992

Papaw and John Morgan, July 2002

Sean, Papaw and Andrew, December 2002

Sean, Andrew, Justin and John Morgan

Trust in the Lord with all your heart,
And lean not to your own understanding.

In all your ways acknowledge Him,
And He shall direct your paths.

Proverbs 3:5-6

Fifteen

Frustration and Fear
Sunday, October 5, 2003

Bill and I have been married forty-six years today. It could very well be the last anniversary we will celebrate. We did not do anything special except to go to church, and then out to dinner at Bill's favorite Mexican restaurant. In spite of Bill's general weakness and problems getting around, he managed to shop for an anniversary card. He never fails to give me a greeting card for my birthday or other special holidays. He usually places them in some conspicuous place around the house, so I will be sure to find them. Sometimes, he would not remember the card until the very last minute. I always knew he had forgotten when he would get up early on that particular day, and he would dress quietly in the dark to keep from waking me. I would hear his truck's motor start before he drove off on his way to the drugstore's greeting card section. The greeting cards usually contain very meaningful verse, and it is obvious that he reads and chooses them carefully. Most of the cards he has given me over the years I have saved—packed away in a drawer. I will always remember and cherish these special things about my husband.

Wednesday, October 8, 2003

Yesterday, good friend Buster drove Bill to the ALS clinic for his monthly appointment. I do not know what we would do without good, caring friends. He did not see the clinic doctor on this visit, but he underwent the usual breathing and exercise testing. For the first time, he required transportation by wheelchair because he was unable to walk the short distances between the hospital departments. My heart fell and my hopes crumbled when he told me about the test results. The exercise test had showed decreased tolerance, and the breathing test (FVC or Forced Vital Capacity) had dropped from an initial level of 78 percent to a current level of 69 percent. I had previously understood the nurse to say that the average normal predicted values for FVC range between 80 and 100 percent.

For several months, Bill has been using a breathing apparatus to exercise the lungs. Its purpose is to strengthen the lungs and keep lung function stable. At first, he could inhale and reach an acceptable 2000-2500 ml mark on the device, but recently he does well if he can reach the 1000-1500 ml mark. I was disappointed but not surprised by the decline in his lung function and strength. Today, he could not lift the usual bag of garbage from the back of his truck onto the dumpster. He told me to use smaller bags for collecting the garbage, and he planned to look into hiring a garbage service.

During an ALS clinic visit, the nurse clinician will usually have Bill complete an ALS Functional Rating Scale (ALSFRS) form. The instructions from the nurse were that the rating scale, used in clinical trials and patient treatment, is a commonly accepted standard for monitoring disease progression. It is used to access the activities of daily living (ADL) for patients with ALS. The patient is to respond by checking or circling the number (on a 0-5 point scale) under each of the twelve activities of daily living, which applies to his/her current level of function or situation. When the patient checks number four under a function, this signifies the function is normal. The responses to all of the functions provide a total. If all functions were normal, the total score would be 48. As function declines, the total score begins to fall. I have become very familiar with the Functional Rating Scale. Because Bill has trouble holding a pencil, I will ask his opinion about the functions and make the appropriate checks on the form.

I began to keep a monthly rating scale for Bill in July of this year. I felt it might help me anticipate his needs by determining what may happen next. Equipment and various assist devices are available to order so ALS patients can live with more ease and safety, but delivery could take several weeks to months. It is important to me for Bill to have whatever he needs in order to live comfortably. I noted at the end of September that his rating scale showed speech disturbance, occasional choking, slow handwriting, some problems cutting food, needing some assistance with dressing, problems climbing stairs, and shortness of breath on exertion. His total score is now 36. I have not told Bill I am keeping the rating scale record. I do not want him to worry or become alarmed when the score begins to decline.

Recently, while searching the internet, I came across a personal website of an ALS patient who is now deceased. As I read the account of his struggle, I could not help but be aware that the symptoms he had at nine months are similar to what Bill is currently experiencing. The photographs posted in the last stages of his disease showed the muscle wasting and limb deformities, which occurs in the legs, feet, arms, and hands. His severely emaciated body reminded me of pictures I have seen of starving people in concentration camps. His functional rating scale showed a gradual declining monthly score. At the time of his death, he had a rating scale score of seven. It is heart wrenching to look at the pictures and read his story because the devastated body and the thin, gaunt face that I see belong to my husband. There was no help for this man, and even though research is ongoing, better treatment will not come in time to help Bill. What I have learned lets me know there will be others who may benefit from the research. Many others will one day receive the dreaded diagnosis and find themselves having to deal with the devastating effects of this disease from Hell.

Saturday, October 18, 2003

If it is autumn, it is football time in Tennessee, and Bill is a huge fan of the University of Tennessee's Big Orange team. Most of the time, he watches the game on TV. In the past, he has always been very excited during a game. He acted like a wild man with the yelling, jumping, and loud comments directed at the TV screen. Last week, on a Saturday night, he went to a game at the football stadium with John Holland. He later said that the short distance he had to walk was extremely difficult due to the leg weakness. On most Saturday games, he invites his brothers and a few friends over to our house to watch the game. Several of them have gathered in the living room today waiting for the big game to start. They seem to enjoy the refreshments I prepare and each other's company. Sitting in his chair among his friends, Bill appears withered and frail compared to the other men in the room. He can no longer yell for the team.

I have little interest in football, so I am usually on the computer searching for information on ALS. Today, I found useful information regarding equipment for bathing and toileting. There are also assist devices for eating, drinking, and writing. I believe it is time to get a transport wheelchair, especially for getting to and from the parking lot and the doctor's office. However, Bill is resistant—not willing to give up his independence. On mention of the wheelchair he usually says, "I know I'm slow, but I can still walk." I decided that some decisions relating to his care were going to be up to me, so I ordered a wheelchair. He helped, as much as he could, to assemble the chair when it arrived; then he parked it out of sight in the hall closet.

My sister tells me that I should not discuss wheelchairs and other handicap equipment with Bill. She is afraid it will upset him and remind him too much of all the dreadful things that are going to happen to him. I very much dread these discussions, and I usually delay them as long as possible. However, I am sure he has already pictured in his mind, every kind of dreadful impairment and infirmity that can be associated with this horrendous disease. Bill knows that he will eventually have to depend on various pieces of equipment in order to move about, and to survive. Perhaps it is my nurses training or take-control character, which drives me to plan and stay a step ahead. Otherwise, I fear I might submit to grief and despair, lose purpose, and become unable to function and deal with it all.

Thursday, October 23, 2003

I lie awake at night and occupy many daytime minutes thinking of ways to engage Bill's time and brighten his life. I feel a sense of urgency to do something soon. How rapidly this disease will destroy the nerves that cause his muscles to work effectively is unknown. I do not know how quickly it will strip away his physical function—his ability to walk. He has always wanted to take an excursion on a cruise ship, but I have been concerned that he is not physically able to tolerate the hectic pace of such a trip. We discussed it thoroughly, and he assured me that he would be to handle it. He actually seems excited at the prospect of going somewhere. Kathleen and Manuel say they are eager to go alone with us. Kathleen will take on the tedious task of checking available cruises and making all the necessary arrangements. She is currently busy concentrating on scheduling a ten-day Caribbean cruise for some time in December.

Unexpected problems recently arose related to the upcoming Caribbean cruise. I found out that our insurance does not provide medical coverage outside of the United States. Fortunately, the secondary family plan, which Bill has through work, does provide coverage. We purchased travel insurance, which covers the four of us in case something comes up and we have to cancel. The cruise is still several weeks away, and I am keeping my fingers crossed that Bill's illness will not progress beyond its current state. My prayer is that he will remain strong enough to enjoy getting away and trying to forget his problems for awhile. Bill now admits that purchasing a wheelchair turned out to be a good idea; that it will be helpful on the trip.

Friday, October 31, 2003

Yesterday, Bill saw the neurologist who diagnosed his ALS. He had to walk several long halls in the building, which caused extreme fatigue. As usual, the doctor was direct, thorough, and to the point. After he examined Bill and noted the progressive weakness in his arms, legs, and voice, he went on to say, "I can tell you what will happen next." He expanded his comment by saying that the choking episodes will increase, the effect on swallowing will gradually become severe, and a feeding tube will be necessary. You can only imagine the painful expression on Bill's face and the terror that he must feel in his heart. He must have a picture, bearing his own image, of each gruesome portrayal. However, the doctor did not appear to notice Bill's reaction. He had picked up the Dictaphone and proceeded to dictate all the unpleasant details about the disease progression as it related to Bill's condition—once again in our presence.

To add to all the problems and the chaos, I recently discovered a dime-sized lump in my right breast tissue. At first, I thought it was only a component of scar tissue because it is located at the site of my mastectomy scar of three years ago. However, this is the first time I have noticed it, and it seems unmovable—fixed to the chest wall. I saw my oncologist this week, and he referred me to the surgeon who had performed my mastectomy. The doctor removed the lump and sent it for analysis, but I have not yet received the biopsy results. I have an ominous feeling about the lump. I pray it will be only scar tissue, but if it turns out to be recurrent breast cancer, I will have a complete new set of challenging problems to deal with.

Comparisons, using the ALS functional rating scale, are made with the patient's status prior to the onset of the disease, not with the status at the last visit.

The patient's response (on a 5-point scale) is recorded in relation to the question, "How are you doing?, for each of the functions listed on the scale.

ALS FUNCTIONAL RATING SCALE

1. **SPEECH**
   - 4 normal speech processes
   - 3 detectable speech disturbances
   - 2 intelligible with repeating
   - 1 speech combined with non-vocal communication
   - 0 loss of useful speech

2. **SALIVATION**
   - 4 normal
   - 3 slight, but definite excess saliva in mouth; may have night-time drooling
   - 2 moderately excessive saliva; may have minimal drooling
   - 1 marked excess saliva with some drooling
   - 0 marked drooling; requires constant tissue or handkerchief

3. **SWALLOWING**
   - 4 normal eating habits
   - 3 early eating problems- occasional choking
   - 2 dietary consistency changes
   - 1 needs supplemental tube feedings
   - 0 NPO (exclusively parenteral or enteral feeding)

4. HANDWRITING

- 4   normal
- 3   slow or sloppy; all words are legible
- 2   not all words are legible
- 1   able to grip pen but unable to write
- 0   unable to grip pen

5. CUTTING FOOD AND HANDLING UTENSILS

___with gastrostomy

- 4   normal
- 3   somewhat slow and clumsy, but no help needed
- 2   can cut most foods, although clumsy and slow; some help needed
- 1   food must be cut by someone, but can still feed slowly
- 0   needs to be fed

6. DRESSING AND HYGIENE

- 4   normal function
- 3   independent and complete self-care with effort or decreased efficiency
- 2   intermittent assistance or substitute methods
- 1   needs attendant for self care
- 0   total dependence

7. TURNING IN BED AND ADJUSTING BED CLOTHES

- 4   normal
- 3   somewhat slow and clumsy, but no help needed
- 2   can turn alone or adjust sheets, but with great difficulty
- 1   can initiate, but not turn or adjust sheets alone
- 0   helpless

8. **WALKING**
   - 4 normal
   - 3 early ambulation difficulties
   - 2 walks with assistance
   - 1 non-ambulatory functional movement only
   - 0 no purposeful leg movement

9. **CLIMBING STAIRS**
   - 4 normal
   - 3 slow
   - 2 mild unsteadiness or fatigue
   - 1 needs assistance
   - 0 cannot do

10. **DYSPNEA (shortness of breath)**
    - 4 none
    - 3 occurs when walking
    - 2 occurs with one or more of the following: eating, bathing, dressing (ADL)
    - 1 occurs at rest, difficulty breathing when either sitting or lying
    - 0 significant difficulty, considering using mechanical respiratory support

11. **ORTHOPNEA (difficult breathing while lying flat)**
    - 4 none
    - 3 some difficulty sleeping at night due to shortness of breath. Does not routinely use more than two pillows
    - 2 needs extra pillow in order to sleep (more than two)
    - 1 can only sleep sitting up
    - 0 unable to sleep

12. **RESPIRATORY INSUFFICIENCY (the lungs cannot take in sufficient oxygen and breathing assistance may be required)**
    4   none
    3   intermittent use of BiPAP
    2   continuous use of BiPAP
    1   continuous use of BiPAP during the night and day
    0   invasive mechanical ventilation by intubation or tracheotomy

13. How many years since onset of symptoms? _____

Source: University if Massachusetts Medical School website, Center for Outcomes Research (copyright 1995-2011), The ALS C-A-R-E Program, used by permission (see end notes[1]).

Then you will call upon Me and
go and pray to Me,
And I will listen to you.

And you will seek and find Me
when you search for Me
with all your heart.

Jeremiah 29:12-13

Sixteen

Added Burdens
Tuesday, November 11, 2003

Today, I was back in the oncologist's office, and I have received the results of the recent breast biopsy. The lump removed was the same type of cell as the previous breast cancer. The doctor's diagnosis was, "Recurrent breast cancer with metastasis," which means the cancer has returned and spread. The news has left me numb and worried but not surprised. I was hoping not have to undergo and tolerate the harsh cancer treatment again, but I listened attentively as the doctor explained the recommended treatment. He said I needed six weeks of chemotherapy and one year treatment with a medication he described as an antibody. A series of radiation treatments will follow the chemotherapy. This particular chemo drug works to paralyze the support structure inside the cancer cell. The cell cannot grow and it dies. The antibody is supposed to target certain types of cancer cells, specifically my type, which is estrogen negative. The drug limits the cell's ability to divide and grow. The side effects of the chemo include hair loss, nausea, fatigue, neuropathy, joint and muscle pain, and heart damage. The major side effect of the antibody drug is heart failure.

When I returned home from the oncologist's office, I received news that was even more alarming. The Gastrointestinal doctor's office called the results of a recent CT scan. The doctor said the scan revealed a lesion on my liver and one lung. In order to evaluate the findings, he had scheduled an Ultrasound of my liver. On hearing this news, I was convinced that the cancer has spread to my liver and lungs. A feeling of fear washed over me when I realized that I could die before Bill. He was visibly upset when I told him of my situation. We had a long discussion about what to do about the upcoming cruise. The oncologist had ordered the chemotherapy to start right away, and he said it was best not to miss treatments. I would not be able to tolerate being on a ship if I had nausea or other major side effects. With the first chemotherapy in 2001, my hair had begun to fall out soon after the first treatment. It would not be pleasant to deal with the hair loss being away from home. I feel guilty because I wanted Bill to go on the trip, but we decided it was best to cancel and focus on what is most important—trying to rid my body of the cancer.

Tuesday, November 20, 2003

Bill has been reluctant to discuss it, but I have been searching the internet for information relating to the cost of converting a van into a wheelchair accessible vehicle. I learned that a new van conversion would cost approximately $25,000. This is in addition to the cost of a new van. Vans are available that have already been converted, and I have compiled a list of local dealerships that carry used vans. I am hoping Bill will agree and be able to help me make all the necessary decisions when the time comes. I am nervous because my knowledge and experience of trading or buying a car is nonexistent. I realize this is a minor issue in the overall scope of challenges.

Recently, Bill has expressed a desire to sell our present home and move to a condominium. He worries about maintaining the house and yard when he loses the use of his arms and legs. He is also concerned about the extra work and burden it will place on me when he is no longer here. Bill likes our house, but I have no great fondness for it. The house we built in 1967, raised our sons, and lived in for thirty years, will always be home to me. There are new condominiums currently under construction in our neighborhood. We would be able to add the necessary handicap features, but I am not sure that this would be the best thing to do. I became more convinced after we toured the place a few days ago. The units are expensive and do not have windows in places that would allow Bill to sit and look outside. The views from the back where windows are located overlook a highway. The rooms are small, gloomy, and overall depressing. Bill told the real estate agent about his illness. I heard him say, "I have a disease that will cause me to be paralyzed, and it will probably kill me before long." The woman's surprised expression and demeanor were obvious as she searched for the right words to say. I have spent the past few days attempting to convince Bill we need to stay where we are. He would be able to move about in most of the house in his wheelchair, and even in the yard if the wheelchair were electric. There is a nice view of the neighborhood, which lies in a country-like setting, and he would have easy access to most windows, the garage, driveway, and back deck. We can hire someone for the yard maintenance as many elderly people do. I am sure Bill realizes it, but I reminded him that neither of us is physically able to undertake the major task of packing and moving. I am hoping he will abandon this idea of moving into a condo.

Saturday, November 29, 2003

Everyday occurrences do not fail to remind us of the heartache we are facing. One day recently, we went to a studio for a family portrait. The setting took a while because little Andrew was busy running around having fun. We were finally able to get him to settle down long enough for the photo shoot to be completed. I knew Bill had been dreading this day. He asked me if we arranged the portraits because he was going to die. As we were preparing to leave he said, "I'll never be in another family photograph—this will be the last one." There was another incident a few nights ago when we went out to dinner with two couples who are our close friends. One friend told of a man that he knows who has ALS. He said the man was able to go on vacation tours two years ago, but now he is on a ventilator. Attempting reassurance, someone else told of another man who has had the disease for fifteen years, but he continues to be able to function fairly well. As I listened to the conversations, I noticed Bill had become unusually quiet, and I wondered what he was thinking. I am sure it reminded him of his own fate. Finally, in an attempt to disguise his true feelings, he broke his silence with a witty remark.

Different people do not always handle life's adversities in the same manner. I cannot predict how Bill will respond as the disease continues to rob his body of its vital functions—when he can no longer walk or talk. I am sure it will be according to his individual values, beliefs, and especially his faith. Most people have heard of the brilliant Physicist and Cosmologist, Stephen Hawking, a scientist well known for his theoretical work on black holes in the Universe. He was only twenty-one when he received the diagnosis of ALS. During his infrequent TV appearances, he seems to be totally paralyzed and is ventilator dependent. He uses a communication device attached to a computer for speaking. However, the illness has not prevented him from lecturing and being active in his work. In a book written about his life, he believed there was nothing to live for following his diagnosis. He eventually realized that if he was going to die anyway, he might as well do something worthwhile.[1] I could not help but wonder if his amazing contributions to science would have occurred had he not been stricken with this ominous disease.

Sometimes, a person responds to adversity with an intense desire to escape it, especially a death sentence from a fatal illness. A TV program that Bill and I watched together a few years ago comes to mind. A national television show aired a video depicting Doctor Jack Kevorkian, sometimes known as Doctor Death, injecting an ALS patient with a lethal substance. The man was in the final stages of the disease, and he had given consent to the assisted suicide in order to end his suffering. In the complicated trial following the man's death, the courts tried and convicted the doctor with second-degree homicide. He began serving the ten to twenty-five year sentence in 1999[2]. As we sat watching the TV program, Bill made an unforgettable comment, "I would rather be dead than live like that." He went on to say, "If I had an awful disease like ALS, I would kill myself." I remember being very distressed by his reaction. As I watched the haunting scene, the commentary made it clear that ALS was a relatively rare disease. The probability that Bill would one day have an illness such as this was highly unlikely. I was not worried about him having ALS, but it was very disturbing to me that he would consider taking his life under any circumstances. My response to his statement was, "God gives us suffering for a reason, and with His help we are expected to bear it." I reminded him that how we handle life's adversities sets an example for other people in our life. Taking his own life was not a legacy he would wish to leave for his children and grandchildren. I am not aware if Bill has considered or had thoughts of suicide since his diagnosis, or if he has changed his mind since our long ago discussion. I do not know, and I have been unable to find the courage to ask.

In spite of the uncertainty and fear, I have much to be thankful for and much to pray for. I pray I will be able to tolerate the cancer treatments, and that they will be effective. I pray Bill will be able to stay at home by himself during my treatments. I pray I will be able to bear the added burden of cancer, and live long enough and be physically able to take care of him. At least, I have a chance at life, but Bill must wake up every day to the realization of his impending death. Every day he must revisit thoughts of the suffering he must endure before a slow but certain death will provide blessed relief. It is possible to hate a disease.

Our home built in 1967
The house where Bill Jr., and John grew up

And it shall come to pass,
That before they call
I will answer;
And while they are yet speaking,
I will hear.

Isaiah 65:24

Seventeen

Cancer Care
Tuesday, December 2, 2003

The sign, CANCER CARE, looms over the doorway of the cancer treatment center. I can recall a time when the sign was very menacing and heart wrenching, but now it has a much different meaning—it signifies hope. I had hoped and prayed never to have to pass through these doors again, but I am here today to begin my fourth week of chemotherapy. As I follow the oncology nurse down the long hallway to the cancer treatment room, memories of that first traumatic experience with cancer, in December of 2000, come rushing back. Like many people, cancer was something that happened to my patients and others but not likely to me. I was very pleased to be in relatively good health as I reached my sixty-fifth birthday. Having medical knowledge and understanding of the importance of annual mammograms and routine medical checkups, I had not been neglectful in this regard. In fact, I completed my annual physical with a breast examination a few months before they found the cancer. The growth was moderately large for a breast tumor, more than three centimeters in size, but both the family physician and I had failed to discover it.

The cancer treatment room is quiet large. A partial wall divides the room where the nurse's station is located. Several recliners, arranged in a circle around the room, provide comfort for patients while they receive treatment. There is an equipment cabinet and an IV stand beside each recliner. The patients who occupy the recliners range from young adult to various stages of older age. As usual, the nurses are very busy. Sometimes the treatment room is so busy patients must receive treatment in the office spaces—even the doctor's office. Some of the patients are obviously very sick, but others have no signs of illness, which causes me to wonder why they are here. Some of the women wear hats or turbans on their heads, others have wigs on, and a few have nothing covering their baldheads. There are several men receiving treatment for cancer this time. Over the past several weeks, I have met patients with a diagnosis of prostate cancer, colon cancer, multiple myeloma, breast cancer, and various other forms of the disease. One woman is in the fight of her life in a battle against lung cancer. The cancer has currently spread to her brain.

This is not a happy place to be, but the nurses try very hard, in spite of the wretchedness, to maintain an upbeat and cheerful environment. They make me proud of my profession. In addition to administering the various chemotherapy drugs, which can be quiet time consuming and complicated, they provide snacks, warm blankets, and are always prepared with emotional support and words of encouragement. Occasionally, I overhear a phone conversation. The nurse tells the patient or caregiver on the other end of the line, "It's probably time to start the morphine." This lets me know that someone has probably begun the terminal stage of some type of cancer.

Last week, when I arrived in the waiting room and sat down, I noticed a young man who appeared to be a teenager sitting near the door. His appearance was curious because he had covered his head with the hood of his jacket, and it hid most of his face. He kept his head covered when it came his turn to go back for treatment. At first, I thought thinning hair was the reason for his actions, or maybe it was his way of escaping reality. I felt much compassion for this young man, and I felt less sorry for myself and my own circumstances. I wished there was something I could do for him, but I did not know what to do or say, so I asked the Lord to watch over him. I have not been able to erase his heartbreaking image from my mind.

Thursday, December 18, 2003

The first time I had cancer I was worried, and I was angry with myself. Being a nurse, I could not believe I had failed to discover the breast mass. I was exceedingly distraught the first time I lost my hair. My hair was thick with a natural curl and has always been my best feature. I can understand when breast cancer patients say their hair loss was almost as traumatic as the loss of the breast. For me, hair loss was a label—a statement that I was a person with cancer. I truly dreaded losing my hair again because dealing with wigs is not pleasant. My hair was thinner when it grew back before, and I can imagine it will be even more straggly now. This time, my hair began to come out about ten days after the first chemo treatment. At first, the hair became very dry, and it came out easily with the use of a brush or comb. I contemplated on whether I should have it completely shaved.

One night, about two weeks ago, I pulled on a section of hair in the front, and it came out in my hand. I found that other sections were loose and would come out easily when pulled. In frustration, I grabbed most of the remaining hair by the handfuls and pulled it out, and I used the scissors to cut off the rest. I put on a wig so Bill would not notice what I had done, and I did not tell him. The first time I lost my hair, it was blonde in color, and I wore blonde wigs. When my hair grew back, it was gray. I had stopped coloring my hair, so I changed to gray wigs. The grandchildren thought the blonde wigs were hilarious, and they would put them on, run around, and laugh at each other. The grown up boys also had fun with the blonde wigs. My having to wear a wig does not have the same bothersome significance as before. When I look at my balding head, I am sure that it is without doubt the very least of my concerns.

Bill and our good friend, Buster, took the monthly trip to the ALS clinic the first week in December. Bill told me he had a difficult time with the testing. It was especially disappointing to hear that his breathing capacity (FVC) had declined even more. He could not remember the exact number, but he vaguely recalled that it was somewhere around 60 percent. One day recently, as he was reading the local newspaper, he read about a local man in his thirties who had died from ALS. Since then, he has become unusually quiet and somber. I know he has withdrawn into gloomy thoughts when he does not talk to me; when he sits for long periods staring at the television screen or out into space. Every time I look upon Bill's sad, downcast face, I wish I could do something to ease his despair. But reality tells me that depression and despair are not all he must deal with. The strength in his legs seems to have worsened overnight. He must have a shopping cart to lean on when he goes into a store. If we go shopping in a store that does not provide carts, he waits in the car. I have encouraged him to use a cane, but he has been resistant. He will say "I don't need one yet." Yesterday, he came home with a collapsible cane, but he has not used it. Maybe it has something to do with pride, but it is more likely an unwillingness to accept what is happening to his body—to his life.

Wednesday, December 24, 2003

Thanksgiving has come and gone, and we have been trying to prepare for the Christmas season. We have a nine-foot artificial tree, and I knew Bill would be unable to help me put it together and set it in place as he has always done. He takes pleasure in decorating the outside of the house with numerous lights, and he arranges his three, lighted, metal deer with care on the front lawn. When the lights are on at night, he is very proud of how great it all looks. This year, he cannot carry the deer from the basement by himself. Bill, Jr., helped his dad put up the outside wreaths and some of the lights. We decided on a smaller tree that I could manage to decorate by myself. If we did not have the children and grandchildren to bless our lives this holiday season, we would indeed be buried in our sorrow.

Sometimes, even as Christians, we tend to forget God's kindness and the blessing He bestows every day. Being very close to this present tragedy, it feels like the worst of all troubles, and I have wanted God to provide the answers that I desired. I asked Him to prevent Bill's ALS diagnosis, but He did not. I prayed for healing, but healing has not occurred. Finally, I prayed the disease would show signs of slowing or remission, but the ALS has a tight grip, and it continues to wreck havoc on his body. As a Christian, I know I am to thank God for the good and the bad; knowing that He uses our troubles to strengthen our faith. As this New Year dawns, even in the midst of tragedy, I hope to have a more thankful heart. I am thankful for family, friends, and neighbors. I am thankful for the necessities of life, medical care, and cancer care. I am especially thankful for Christ and for God's promise that He will not leave us to bear the weight of this terrible burden alone.

Bill and John goofing off with the wigs in happier times

Sean and Andrew playing with Mammaw's wigs

Thus says the Lord, your Redeemer,
The Holy One of Israel:
I am the Lord your God,
Who teaches you to profit,
Who leads you by the way
you should go.

Isaiah 48:17

Eighteen

God is Still at Work
Friday, January 4, 2004

Christmas has come and gone, and a New Year has begun. I have a feeling it will be a trying one. The grim news that the CT scan revealed lesions on my liver and lung has been a source of great concern and a dark cloud hanging over our heads. I wanted to see the report for myself, so while at work one day, I pulled it up on the computer. The radiologist's summary interpretation was, "Breast cancer with probable metastasis to the liver and lung." During my nursing career, metastasis was always a dreaded and an ominous word to see on any report. It means the cancer has spread to other parts of the body. I have been reading reports such as these for many years; they are seldom in error. The oncologist, wanting to be sure, arranged for a full body scan, and I prepared for the worst. I was surprised when the doctor called to say the scan was negative, showing no signs that the cancer had spread. The lung lesion turned out to be scar tissue, and the liver lesion was gallstones. God is still at work.

I thought I had learned more about this disease called ALS than I ever wanted to know, but it's debilitating, treacherous effects still catch me by surprise. I was aware that the neck muscles could become too weak to support the head. In this case, a neck brace may be required. Hand splints are sometimes necessary because of muscle weakness in the hands and fingers. Weakened muscles in the feet can cause a pulling down on the foot, which can lead to foot drop. Foot drop is the inability to lift or flex the foot. Ankle-foot braces are available for this condition. In fact, muscles around any joint can weaken; leading to the need for a variety of braces or supports to assist with function and comfort.[1] I had not previously considered back problems in the overall scope of disabilities. I became aware of the problem when Del was helping Bill take down the outside Christmas lights, I noticed that his back was bowed and he slumped over while walking. I quickly realized this indicates deterioration of the back and abdominal muscles. We obtained a back brace, but it placed pressure on his abdomen and chest, which resulted in more difficult breathing. He tried the brace several times, but could not tolerate it. Reluctantly, but by necessity, he was finally convinced he must use a cane for walking or risk a fall. One day, he had a need to go into the storage space over our garage, but he could only manage the first three steps on the ladder. I will never forget his tortured expression as he backed off the ladder and turned in my direction. It was all I could do to control my emotions and keep from crying.

Friday, January 9, 2004

We saw Bill's primary physician today. The doctor told us he was obviously weaker, and he was concerned about the continued weight loss. He said we would have to make a decision about a feeding tube before long. He inquired about Bill's feelings regarding a ventilator when it becomes necessary, and asked if he had thought about suicide. Bill responded by saying, "I have no plans to kill myself." Regarding the ventilator, he told the doctor, "I don't want to be placed on a ventilator as stated in my Living Will." The doctor explained that in case of an acute illness or choking, a ventilator might be required on a temporary basis. He said Bill could make a decision later as to whether he wanted to continue its use. I left the office in a state of confusion. If Bill needed a ventilator for an acute situation, weaning him off would be unlikely due to his diminished lung capacity. It would be a tough decision on whether to remove it. It has been my experience that once a patient is on a ventilator, the decision to remove it becomes very difficult and can be complicated. Bill has already decided he does not want a ventilator, and he has said more than once that he would rather die quickly. I am very concerned that the doctor's statement about the temporary use of the ventilator will cause him to become confused about his decision. If he is unsure about what to do, he will want to leave the decision up to me as he often does in medical matters. Somehow, he has to understand that the use of the ventilator is one decision he alone must make.

Sunday, January 18, 2004

It seems Bill's speech has become worse overnight. I notice that servers at restaurants have problems understanding what he says when he places an order. I will often order for him, or I must repeat what he has said. I make it a point to go along when we want fast food because he becomes so frustrated. Friends and family members have also recognized that his speech is becoming worse. He will say, "I can't understand why people have such a problem with my speech." Lately, I have noticed that his hand movements are less coordinated, and he drops things more often than usual. His typical smooth, precise handwriting is jagged, uneven, and becoming difficult to read. We went to dinner after church today, and he overturned a glass of tea at the restaurant. He attempted to make light of it at the time, but he has been noticeably upset and irritable all afternoon.

The nutritional problems and continued weight loss have gradually become a major concern. Bill weighed 192 pounds when he received the ALS diagnosis in January of 2003. He currently weighs 165 pounds. It is becoming more and more difficult to plan a meal because food no longer appeals to him, and the chemotherapy has a negative effect on my own appetite. No matter what food I prepare, he eats very little. Regarding most foods, he will say, "Everything tastes the same—like cardboard." I offer him milk shakes and other high caloric beverages, but milk products cause gas and abdominal distention. He declines any food that has an effect to increase the abdominal pressure because it makes breathing more difficult. He believes his poor appetite is due to all the medication he must take every day, and I believe he is correct. The primary physician recommended he try an over-the-counter medication, which is often used to improve the appetite in older people. He tried the tonic for a while, but it did not help. I recently purchased a food chopper/blender with the idea that I could mash, grind, or puree many of the foods he likes for easier swallowing consistency. I am sitting here tonight making a list of foods to prepare; foods I hope he will be able to swallow and tolerate well enough to maintain his weight.

Scrambled eggs	creamed soups	fruit cobbler
grits	creamed potatoes	ice cream
oatmeal	cream corn	plain cake
cream of wheat	peas	Jell-o
pancakes	pinto beans	yogurt
applesauce	sweet potatoes	puddings
bananas	asparagus	fruit smoothie
cottage cheese	macaroni	canned fruit
strawberries	chili	Italian ice
spoon bread	beef stew	cream pies
pasta/sauce	ground meat/gravy	custards
rice	chicken/dumplings	fruit nectars

Friday, January 29, 2004

By now, I have completed several chemotherapy treatments, and I am beginning to experience the bothersome side effects. In addition to nausea and loss of appetite, I have mouth sores, numbness and tingling in my fingers and toes, and joint and muscle pain. The pain makes it difficult to sleep at night, and I am often irritable. I sometimes find myself losing patience with Bill, and this hurts my heart. While doing household chores, I must stop and rest due to fatigue. Bill attempts to help me, but he is now so weak and short of breath, he can accomplish very little. He tells me that he feels so worthless.

The cancer treatments, scheduled on Tuesday of each week, require approximately four hours for the administration of the drug. It takes a couple of days to obtain relief from the worst side effects. Due to fatigue and weakness, working at the hospital has become a difficult challenge. The doctor also warned that I needed to be careful about exposure to patients who may have an infection. The chemotherapy drug can lower the white blood cell count compromising the immune system. This leaves me at risk for contacting an infection. After some soul searching and considering Bill's condition, I recently decreased my workdays to two days a month. The two days is the minimum required to remain actively employed. I keep little Andrew two days a week while his mother works as an elementary school teacher. A week can go by very quickly, but the worry and concern regarding the coming weeks and months constantly occupy my thoughts.

Bill is not relinquishing his independence easily. He does what he can for himself and asks for help only as a last resort. He uses a stool in the shower and must sit down even when he shaves or brushes his teeth. I notice that he is having difficulty climbing into the driver's seat of his truck. He does not go away from home as often as he did, and he seems to choose the places he goes with care. Everyday activities are becoming more of a problem. Last week, he went to the local garage to put air in the tires of my car. When he came home, he told me that his fingers were so weak he could not press and hold the air hose down. I had to go back with him later that day in order to complete the task. Following an occurrence such as this, he usually sinks into a gloomy state. I am sure he must be feeling helpless and hopeless. His determined efforts are hard to watch.

I am surprised but proud of the way Bill has dealt with ALS this first year. He is usually a person that does not handle illness well. In the past a bad cold could be about as much as he could tolerate. We both have reason to dread this upcoming year because it is obvious that the losses in physical function are occurring at a faster pace. It seems as if new changes occur overnight. Bill has put a lot of faith in the clinical trial medication, but if he is receiving the actual Celebrex drug, it is not working. When I look at the functional rating scale that I keep for my own records, I am sad and discouraged. At the end of November, his functional rating scale score was 35 (his beginning score was 48). The New Year of 2004 began with a score of 33. Bill has fought hard not to become disabled, or appear to be limited in some way. He does not know a lot about the physiology of ALS, but I am confident he realizes that he is getting worse and not better. As we go forward into this New Year, I believe we are both realizing that the actual hard struggle with this disease is just beginning.

Come to Me, all you who labor and
are heavy laden,
and I will give you rest.

Take My yoke upon you and learn from Me,
For I am gentle and lowly in heart,
and you will find rest for your souls.

Matthew 11:28-29

Nineteen

Acceptance
Thursday, February 5, 2004

There seems to be an unusually high incidence of hearing loss among Bill's fellow firefighters. A few months ago, we learned that several firefighters were exploring initiating legal proceedings related to this. The suit claims that the hearing loss is due to damage from frequent on-the-job exposure to high frequency alarms, bells, and loud sirens. The firefighters had not previously been required to wear hearing protective devices. Those affected were not only retired firefighters, but some still actively employed. The legal issue focuses on obtaining hearing evaluations and hearing aids for those determined to have hearing loss related to their job as a firefighter. Bill began to lose hearing early in his career, and the problem has worsened over the years. Today, he has moderate to severe hearing loss. Hearing aids can cost $3,000 each, so Bill was eager to place his name on the claims list. When he first learned of the legal plans, the effects of ALS on his physical function were somewhat mild. After the court dates were set up he decided, "If I'm going to die, I won't need hearing aids." I was concerned and felt it would be important, especially if he lost speech, to be able to hear well. He finally agreed to the hearing aids, but he did not have them when we went to court for the first time the last week in January. Our dependable friend, Buster, drove us to the courthouse and helped me to take Bill from place to place in his wheelchair. We were disappointed to learn that they had postponed the trial until the end of February. The trip to the courthouse was difficult for Bill. I hope he will be strong enough to withstand future trips; that his speech will not deteriorate and prevent him from being able to testify effectively.

It seems there is no end to dealing with problems. Bill recently received a letter from the Social Security Administration (SSA). It seems there was an overpayment of benefits for 2001. The notification was to remind him that they would deduct the overpayment amount from his current monthly check. I attempted to intercede for him in this matter by phone. They told me I would need to apply and receive an authorized assignment to be his designated representative payee. In addition, the attending physician would need to submit a letter describing Bill's illness and physical condition. This would allow me to conduct Social Security business on his behalf. Last week, I went to the local Social Security Administration office to complete an application to be Bill's representative payee and to show reason why he needed assistance to conduct his business affairs. If approved, I will be able to sign his name, cash his checks, and speak for him when he can no longer write or speak. I will be able to use his SS benefits on his behalf, but I must keep records and submit an annual report to the SSA as to how I used the money. In the gigantic arsenal of government red tape, I am sure there must be good reasons for these strict rules. We already have this terrible disease to deal with, and I would prefer not to have to cope with the additional stress related to this matter. Trouble continues to come in clusters and layers.

Friday, February 13, 2004

Friday 13 is not an ideal day to finalize your federal income tax returns. However, Bill and I went to have our taxes completed for 2003. He has always kept the necessary records for our taxes, had knowledge of the required documentation, and compiled the necessary information for the professional tax service to complete. This year, he has left most everything to me. I believe he is preparing me for when I will have to do it on my own. I did not have a clue as to where to start, but with his help, I finally figured it out. After completing the taxes, we went to Bill's favorite Mexican restaurant. He seemed to enjoy his food, and I thought it to be odd that he can tolerate this spicy food so well. After the meal, however, he was so fatigued he had difficulty getting back to the car using his cane. I believe the cane is becoming an insufficient means of support. It is also obvious that he will need to stop driving soon, and he will not accept it graciously.

Like many men and boys, Bill has a genuine affection for motor vehicles. His first car was a 1952 green Oldsmobile. After he graduated from high school, he went to Michigan with a friend and worked in a steel factory for a couple of years. He purchased the Oldsmobile with the money he saved. Bill wore his hair in the Elvis ducktail hairstyle, which was popular among the young men in the fifties and sixties, and he thought he was cool driving around town in that car. He still talks fondly about his green Olds. In the early years of our marriage, he was partial to Oldsmobile cars, but over the years, he has preferred to drive a truck. His best loved GMC Sierra, damaged by the hailstorm and restored to its original condition, looks as good as new, and he takes meticulous care of it. He gets upset if he notices the least scratch or dent, and he keeps a coordinating silver paint handy just for covering scratches. He has now become unable to hold the small paintbrush, or steady his hand well enough to apply the paint to the scratches. When there are touch-ups to do, he sits on a rolling utility cart and rolls around the truck in order to point out the areas he wants me to paint. My efforts do not always meet his expectations. You can imagine my surprise when he told me, "I'm thinking about selling my truck."

Bill enjoys driving. During trips we have taken, it seems he can drive forever without stopping. He likes to go places he has never been. He especially likes to drive in the country and rural areas. Sometimes, on a Sunday afternoon, he would take me for a drive. The places we went were so unfamiliar I would think we were lost, but he always managed to find the main highway. Lately, Bill has been unable to climb onto the seat of the truck, but he still insists on driving. He uses his cane to get to the truck, and then he holds onto the garage wall to open the door. I have to boost him up onto the seat. When he is out driving, he does not get out of the truck because he is afraid of falling. Every time I watch him drive away, I get a surge of anxiety and a heavy feeling in my chest. I worry he might have an accident, and I wonder if his feet and legs are strong enough to operate the gas and brakes appropriately. If I ask him where he has been after one of his driving excursions, he will usually say something like, "I was just driving around—thinking." When I know Bill is out driving by himself, I get a picture of a frail, tortured human being driving alone down a country road. He is carrying a burden on his soul that one can only imagine. I believe he is attempting to experience as much as he can of the mountains, lakes, and other places that he loves; while there is still time.

Wednesday, February 18, 2004

Last week, we bought a 2002 Buick Rendezvous minivan. Today, Bill sold his truck to Bill, Jr. We could use the money from the sale of the truck toward the purchase of the van, but I encouraged him to keep the truck and drive it as long as possible. He told me, "It doesn't matter; I can no longer keep it cleaned and serviced as I should." I am saddened because I can tell the decision breaks his heart. I believe Bill's letting go of his truck is a beginning sign of acceptance of the inevitable. It would be only the first of many losses to come. We did not need two vehicles, so I gave my Oldsmobile Aurora to my sister, Jean, who needed a car. Jean and my niece, Elaine, came from Erwin on Saturday to pick up the Oldsmobile. They were aware of Bill's illness, but had not seen him since last April. It was shocking for them to see how sick he looks; how thin and frail. They both went out of his sight and hearing into the kitchen and broke down in tears.

Even though Bill says that before long, he won't be able to walk or do anything else, he continues to avoid discussions regarding a handicapped vehicle. It has been difficult to make him understand that I must arrange for his transportation to and from the doctors' offices and the ALS clinic. I think he resists because he is not prepared to accept a handicap label. I was relieved when he finally agreed and was physically able to help me choose a van. I did not feel capable of doing it on my own. I have never driven a large vehicle before, and learning to drive; especially to park the van will be my next immediate challenge. The next step will be to find out how to get the van restructured to accommodate a wheelchair. I am relieved about the van, but I sometimes feel guilty and wonder if I am pushing Bill to make decisions and do things against his will. I do not want to add to his anguish, but I do not know what else to do.

Many people cope with trouble and problems by sharing their feelings and concerns with others, but this is not in Bill's character. After a year of no improvement in his condition, only worsening, he must feel unbearably hopeless. He takes antidepressant medication, but his sadness seems so great at times, I wish it were possible for me to bear his suffering. The ALS Association's Coping with Change manual reports that sadness is a normal response to a devastating illness, "There can be anguish to this disease, which encompasses the soul."[1] Every now and then, I get a picture in my mind of Bill being totally paralyzed, with his mind locked in a body that is unable to move, speak, or wipe a tear from his eye. The vision is very painful, and my mind cannot grasp it for long. This state of helplessness has been his greatest fear. By now, we both realize nothing can stop the onslaught of this menacing disease. The decision to give up his truck is a strong but sure sign that he is beginning to accept and let go.

I have witnessed death when it comes suddenly and painlessly; but also when it has a gradual yet expected arrival. But most of us are denied that sudden, sure death. Either way, death is an unwanted visitor, which brings with it an unwelcome ending. Death usually involves a difficult struggle, which is accompanied by uncertainty and fear of the unknown. There is a natural resistance to accept one's own demise; to acknowledge that everything you have been or have known in life is coming to an end. It has been my experience as a nurse that there comes a time when that inborn nature to do everything you can to survive dissipates; when hope is discarded, and the pathway toward acceptance begins. Recent events tell me that Bill has reached this point in his journey. One day he asked me to gather his gold and diamond jewelry. He did not have a lot, but he wanted our sons to have it and to choose which pieces they wanted. A few weeks later, he gave the boys several guns he had collected over the years. The actual scenes during the giving, Bill trying to maintain composure and hold back tears, and the sorrowful expression on each son's face was heartbreaking to watch. Having relinquished his possessions, I knew that Bill, having abandoned all hope, had crossed over into complete acceptance of his impending death.

*And He said to me, "My grace
is sufficient for you,
My strength is made perfect
in weakness."*

2 Corinthians 12:9

Twenty

Sustaining Grace
Monday, March 4, 2004

Bill's legs have become so weak; he must always use the wheelchair when we go anywhere. When we traveled to the ALS clinic in February for his scheduled appointment, the wheelchair was a tremendous help to prevent him from becoming extremely fatigued. Following the battery of tests at the clinic, the nurse told us that his breathing capacity (FVC) was 41 percent. This was a decrease from the initial 78 percent, and it indicates further weakness of the muscles that assist breathing. My heart sank when I heard this, for I have read when the FVC nears a 30 to 35 percent range, the patient may need the use of a ventilator in order to survive. The ALS clinic doctor strongly advised Bill to begin using a breathing assist device called BiPAP (Bi-Level Positive Air Pressure). I was to select a local home equipment company and let the clinic nurse know which company was to receive the doctor's orders. After we returned home that day, Bill was so discouraged and weary; he went directly to bed. The reality that he already needs breathing assistance was so unexpected and devastating; I went outside alone in the dark and cried very bitter tears.

I was familiar with the CPAP (Continuous Positive Airway Pressure), a common treatment for obstructive sleep apnea, but I was not familiar with the BiPAP. I had to refer to the ALS Association's Living with ALS manual. A BiPAP is a lightweight, small, portable, ventilation support system, which uses electronic circuits to monitor the patient's breathing. Tubing connects the machine to either a facemask or a device, which fits into the nose called nasal pillows. The machine delivers two levels of pressure to the lungs. It delivers a higher level during inspiration and a lower level during expiration. The BiPAP only supports or assists breathing when the patient is unable to breathe effectively. It can facilitate comfort by decreasing the work of breathing. The BiPAP, designed specifically for mask or nasal pillow application, functions as a non-life-support system for adult patients. It does not prevent the progression of ALS.[1]

The disease does not affect the lungs themselves, but the nerves that control the respiratory muscles. The nerve destructive process affects the diaphragm and other muscles in the chest that assist to pump air in and out of the lungs. These muscles become progressively weak and strained and are unable to expand the lungs. Eventually, the patient is unable to maintain an adequate level of breathing, which can lead to respiratory failure and respiratory crisis. Weakened chest muscles can also lead to decreased cough strength and the inability to clear secretions from the respiratory tract. If an ALS patient gets even a mild respiratory tract infection, the retained secretions cause breathing to become more difficult and oxygen levels fall. This leads to an increased risk for pneumonia. A diagnosis of pneumonia for an ALS patient is serious and usually requires hospitalization.[2]

The disease process can also lead to deterioration of the muscles required for swallowing. Inability to swallow effectively may cause food, liquids, and saliva to drop down into the bronchial tree and lungs resulting in aspiration pneumonia. During a person's sleep, as a normal occurrence, breathing muscles relax and breathing becomes shallow. With ALS, the additional muscle weakness affects the ability to maintain an open airway. This can lead to snoring, noisy breathing, or breathing, which may be intermittently blocked or stopped.[3]

Sunday, March 7, 2004

As Bill's care needs increase, I must interact with various medical facilities and equipment companies. I am learning that many people who work in health care are unfamiliar with ALS and its effects. The home equipment company had received the BiPAP prescription. The representative told me that Bill had to have a sleep study. During the study, he must demonstrate at least thirty episodes where he stopped breathing in order to meet the strict insurance coverage guidelines. Following much discussion, I was able to help her understand that stopping breathing was not the problem, but a paralyzed diaphragm and inadequate air exchange. Following several more attempts at clarification, the insurance company did agree to fund the BiPAP for three months. Then, an evaluation to determine if his lungs had improved would be necessary. This decision was irritating and very frustrating. Why would anyone expect the lungs to improve with an ALS diagnosis? It was disturbing to think that treatment denial would occur if there were no signs of lung recovery.

Confusion also arose regarding the cost to rent the machine. The original quote was $265 a month. Later, the equipment company representative changed the quote to $650 a month. Finally, the quote for the total cost to rent the equipment Bill will need was $700 a month. We contemplated buying a machine, and found that a new BiPAP would run approximately $1,800. This would be a gigantic cost savings. It occurred to me; however, that there would be no one available to service a personally owned machine if there were problems. It was a relief to learn that his combined health insurance would cover the cost to rent the BiPAP equipment.

Instructions from the ALS clinic nurse were for Bill to use the BiPAP intermittently in the daytime in order to become accustomed to it. Eventually, the goal is to be able to use it during the entire night. Much to my disappointment, Bill began to have problems with the machine right away. He complained that it caused smothering and nasal congestion. He would put it on for a short while, and then take it off again. We had a few squabbles in the process of my trying to convince him that he had to learn to use the machine as instructed; that his life may depend on it. He would sometimes get irate and, among other things, would call me an "old devil". Once, I lost patience and told him many people have had to learn to use these machines in order to breathe, and he would have to learn. I reminded him that Jim Woody must use a CPAP during the night, and it is a much more difficult machine to tolerate. At the end of the day, we were both haggard and worn from the stress and fatigue of dealing with all the problems. One day, I had him watch a video from the ALS Association called, Adapting to Breathing Changes. The focus, relating to the use of the BiPAP, was that it not only helps breathing, it enhances sleep, improves fatigue, prevents headaches related to carbon dioxide buildup, and may even improve the voice and prolong life.[4] After watching the video, I noticed he wears his mask for longer periods. I am praying that his anxiety will lessen, and that he will be able to adhere to directions for the use of the BiPAP machine.

Monday, March 22, 2004

On February 27, we went back to the courthouse. I have been very concerned about Bill's participation in the trial. His voice is weak and his speech so slurred, I feared he would not be able to testify. He required assistance with the microphone, but he did very well with it held close to his mouth. As I recall, the judge did not ask him to repeat anything he said. The trial process lasted approximately four hours, and he was rather fatigued afterwards. It warmed my heart when I saw him laughing and attempting to make conversation with several of his firefighter friends that he had not seen in a while. As I sat in the courtroom watching him testify, hunched over and straining to speak his loudest, I was taken aback by the drastic change in his appearance. The change appears more obvious in a setting such as this where other people are moving about and talking normally. I am saddened because I know he feels as if everyone is looking at him and feeling sorry for him. My thoughts go back to the time when he was strong, active, and happy. Now he is so frail and weak, he cannot walk to the witness stand or climb into the chair without assistance. I regretted that I encouraged him to take part in the trial.

Early in the month, Bill had an appointment to see the neurologist who diagnosed him. He weighed 155 pounds on the office scales; a drop of 20 pounds in four months. The doctor began by suggesting a feeding tube. Bill avoided by asking him if it was okay to try red wine for his appetite. The doctor gave his permission for the wine, but had no other suggestions for the nutritional problems. He performed the usual examination and noted that Bill's muscles and his voice was weaker overall. He ordered a swallowing exam (a Barium Swallow) to test for swallowing or aspiration problems, and referred him to a speech therapist to evaluate the need for a communication device. Bill realizes his speech is deteriorating. I have noticed that he seldom answers the phone, and when a family member fails to understand something he has said, he ignores any requests to repeat it.

Bill continues to have problems with the BiPAP machine. It is a constant source of irritation. It is bothersome, yet the most critical aspect of his treatment. His face is thinning, and each mask soon becomes too large for his face. He uses a chin and head strap, but the air still escapes around the mask preventing a good seal. This causes the BiPAP to cycle inappropriately and be ineffective. I took him to the home equipment company to see about getting a smaller mask. The insurance guidelines restrict payment to one mask every three months, so we had to pay the cost of $165. In the meantime, the nutrition problem is reaching a crucial level. Bill will insist, "I'm not having a feeding tube," but he eats very little. He cannot bear the smell of food cooking on the stove and says the thought of food causes nausea. He tried the wine, but it did not help. At this point, I am at my wits end and in a quandary as to what to do next.

Tuesday, March 30, 2004

A stomach virus has been going around, and Bill picked it up from somewhere. For several days, he experienced stomach pains, nausea, and diarrhea. He has taken only liquids and the most important of his medications. It is unusual for him to contact an illness in this manner. I am sure his immune system is in a weakened state due to his poor nutrition and lack of essential vitamins and minerals. He will be at risk for any infection, and I must make sure to avoid his exposure to illnesses in the coming months. During this illness, I was anxious and hoping that he would not vomit and aspirate the fluid into his lungs. Thankfully, the illness subsided, but I made plans to rent an oral suction machine to have on hand for times such as this.

With much effort and fortitude, Bill has gradually increased his ability to use the BiPAP machine four to five hours during the day. When he uses it consistently, he has less fatigue, and the pale color of his face improves. However, he still uses the machine only for short periods at night. He puts the mask on when he lies down, but it will soon become dislodged. This sets off the alarm and wakes him. After a few of these episodes, he becomes aggravated, removes the mask, and lays it aside. Unless I stay awake and get up at frequent intervals to replace it, the mask stays off most of the night. It makes sense, for an ALS patient, that elevating the head would decrease pressure on the diaphragm and make breathing easier. I told Bill he would be able to rest better with his head raised, and we needed to get a hospital bed. He refused by saying, "I'm not that sick yet." I finally convinced him to try a twin sized electric bed that we were able to borrow from a friend. The bed had a vibrator, and the head and foot could be adjusted up or down for comfort. To make room for the bed, our bedroom furniture had to be rearranged. Thankfully, I was able to move the furniture by myself. Bill tried his best to help me, but his strength gave out quickly. It broke my heart to see the expression on his face as he sat sadly by and watched me as I struggled to move the heavier pieces of furniture.

As the days and weeks expend themselves, it is obvious that Bill's condition is gradually worsening. He complains of constant, extreme fatigue. He goes to bed much earlier, and he does not hurry to get up in the morning. I suppose sleep can be a welcomed form of escape. Today, I had my weekly chemo treatment, and I am feeling weak and tired. The drugs have resulted to decrease my red blood cell count, and the medication used to restore the count causes aching joints. I will be glad when the chemo treatments end the last of July. Each day, I am still able to be thankful for something. Yesterday, I was thankful to receive a good report from the mammogram of my remaining breast. Today, I had the strength to accomplish the required tasks.

I usually do my thinking and write in the journal after Bill has retired for the evening; when all is calm. Over the past few months, I have developed an immense appreciation for quietness and solitude. In the blessedness of quietness, I am able to clear my head and concentrate on the immediate future. As I write in the journal tonight, the challenges that lay ahead seem impossible, dreadful, and daunting. I will be able to meet them only with the grace and help of God who sustains me.

He Drew Me Away

I needed the quiet so He drew me aside
Into the shadows where we could confide,
Away from the bustle where all the day long
I hurried and worried when active and strong.

I needed the quiet though at first I rebelled
But gently, so gently my cross He upheld
And whispered so gently of spiritual things
Though weakened by body, my spirit took wings
To heights never dreamed of when active and gay
He loved me so gently He drew me away.

I needed the quiet, no prison my bed
But a beautiful valley of blessing instead
A place to grow richer in Jesus to hide,
I needed the quiet, so He drew me aside.

Author unknown

*I will instruct you and teach you
in the way you should go;
I will guide you with My eye.*

Psalm 32:8

Twenty-one

Difficult Decisions
Saturday, April 3, 2004

I was busy in the kitchen this morning when I heard a loud noise. I rushed into the den and found Bill lying face down on the floor. He had tripped and fallen while coming in from the garage. Thankfully, he was not injured. He appeared humiliated when he told me he fell because the bottoms of his house slippers are slick. For the past few weeks, I have noticed a definite change in his walking. He often stumbles for no reason, and he has problems picking up his feet causing a shuffling type gait. Maybe this fall help him realize he can no longer ignore the progressive weakness in his arms and legs.

The trip to the ALS clinic the last of March was miserable. The pouring rain, high volume of traffic, and the many large trucks on the highway made for a nerve-racking experience. Our son, John, drove us there and back on the same day. Adding to my anxiety, John had not slept well the night before, and he had a hard time staying awake. Bill completed the usual battery of tests at the clinic, but the results were not good. His breathing function (FVC) had dropped from 41 percent last month to a current 36 percent. The nurse clinician said it was imperative that he use the BiPAP during the night. She evaluated his physical function, which revealed that he has difficulty getting up from a chair, difficulty turning in bed, extreme fatigue with showering, and he has fallen at least once. He continues to drive my car, but he struggles to get in and out of it. All these show an overall decline in muscle function. Finally, she suggested that we initiate the process of getting a power wheelchair soon. She wrote a prescription for the wheelchair and, at my request, a suction machine. It was not a surprise to learn that Bill's condition is worsening. By now, we have become accustomed to hearing dire or troubling news. Following the initial disappointment and shock, we numbly accept it and try to prepare for whatever will come next.

Swallowing is an automatic function and something we take for granted. The possibility of choking to death is a frightening concept under normal circumstances. Whenever an illness or condition such as ALS dramatically increases the person's chance of choking, it would be understandable why they would hesitate to eat or drink. Yesterday, I took Bill to the outpatient clinic for a swallowing test to determine the extent of his swallowing problems. While we waited for the test results, we expected to hear that it had become one more critical issue. Surprisingly, the doctor told us that Bill's swallowing was almost normal. She provided swallowing tips to prevent choking episodes. She advised Bill to eat slowly, take small bites, swallow two to three times, and take a sip of liquid after each bite. He should swallow with his head level or tipped forward toward the chest. He should keep his lips closed while chewing and never talk while eating. Thicker liquids are easier to swallow than thin liquids, but he should not use straws except with thicker liquids. He is to avoid dry food or any food that is difficult to swallow. She suggested we use a thickening product, which makes all liquids thicker—even water. The doctor seemed optimistic, and she told Bill that a feeding tube could be avoided if he is able to maintain the necessary calories. The Barium Swallow test will need to be repeated in six months.

Monday, April 5, 2004

I submitted my notice to the hospital today, ending a forty-five year nursing career. It will be a big change in my life, but I can no longer leave Bill at home alone. He has not been eating the meals I prepare for him to warm up, and he usually does not drink the nutritional supplements. If it had not been for the help of neighbors who agreed to check on Bill while I was at work, it would have been necessary for me to retire long before now. God sometimes answers prayer and meets our needs through the goodness and kindness of others. I am so thankful for Jim and Nancy, and Del and Drama.

As I think back over my long nursing career, I feel blessed that I was able to work so many years in a profession I love; in a place that provided support and an opportunity to grow. I will greatly miss all the patients, doctors, nurses, and other professionals whom I have worked with over the years. Looking back, I cannot recall a day, unless I was ill, that I did not look forward to going to work. Sometimes, I became so immersed in work, I would forget to pick up my paycheck. Bill thought a dedication such as this bordered on the extreme, and he would tease me about it.

Last week, Bill saw his primary physician. He too concluded that Bill seems, in a general sense, to be much weaker. He had been concerned about a recent elevated blood sugar that has now returned to normal. Thank goodness, we do not have to deal with a diagnosis of Diabetes. During this visit, one of Bill's blood tests revealed an elevated potassium level, and the cause is a mystery. Nevertheless, the doctor gave him a prescription for a potassium lowering medication, and he is to avoid foods containing high levels of the substance. Most of the discussion centered on Bill's weight loss and lack of appetite. The doctor said malnutrition was becoming a very serious problem and once again strongly recommended a feeding tube. Bill continues to say he is not ready for a feeding tube. He assured the doctor that he would try harder to eat and drink. Near the end of the visit, the subject of the ventilator came up again. Bill's response indicated he had given it some thought. He said he would accept a temporary breathing tube in the event of an emergency. Then he told the doctor, "I don't want to depend on a machine in order to live." I am relieved that he has made this important decision on his own, but it is still heart wrenching to hear him speak the words.

It seems one of us is constantly going to the doctor, having some type of test, undergoing a treatment, learning to use a piece of equipment, or taking a new medication. The visit to the speech therapist last week was meaningful yet distressing. Following her evaluation, the therapist recommended we place an order for a speech assist device as soon as possible. She indicated the loss of speech is a foregone conclusion, and it is important for Bill to become familiar with using the device before he loses his speech entirely. The speech equipment, which is computerized, will cost approximately $4,500, but the combination of the two insurances should cover the cost. We were told that the Muscular Dystrophy Association might help, if necessary, with the cost of the machine. As we left the office to return home, Bill made no comment, but I knew he could barely comprehend the thought of having to use a machine for speaking. His functional rating score the first of April was 26. Since his ALS diagnosis, he has lost 50 percent of his motor muscle function. This horrendous disease is taking over too much—too fast.

Tuesday, April 13, 2004

The firefighters won their case related to the hearing loss, but an appeal resulted in a decision reversal. Bill had completed all the hearing tests and the fittings for the hearing aids, and he was patient during the entire process. He was not pleased that we must pay out of pocket for the hearing aids. He still insists, "It's a waste of money to buy hearing aids for someone who is dying." Nevertheless, I was adamant about the hearing aids because I want him to hear well for communication purposes. It would also be important to be able to hear the TV when he becomes home bound. Hearing aids generally cost $3,000 each, but with Buster's assistance, Bill was able to purchase a pair at a much lower cost. Since receiving the hearing aids, the improvement in his hearing has been amazing. Before, he would have to turn the TV volume very high in order to hear it, but now, he is able to hear it at a much lower volume. Sometimes he turns the volume so low, I have trouble hearing it myself.

I have noticed that Bill has a weak, ineffective cough. In spite of his best efforts, he has problems in completely clearing his throat of normal secretions. He can barely blow his nose due to the weakened chest muscles. Coughing is another important function we take for granted. An effective cough requires a big breath in and a rapid breath out. For an ALS patient, a weak cough can lead to serious problems by increasing the risk for aspiration and pneumonia. At my request, after discussing the problem with the doctor, he ordered a cough assist machine. The cough machine is a mechanical device designed to simulate a cough and clear any retained secretions from the throat and lungs. It does this, using tubing and a mouthpiece connected to the machine, by applying positive pressure to the airway in order to load the lungs with a deep breath. It then shifts to a rapid negative pressure for rapid airflow out.[1] Bill has attempted to use the machine several times, but each time the negative pressure functioned to pull the air from his lungs, he would lose his breath for a short period and panic. It caused him so much anxiety; I had no choice but to set the machine aside. He finally told me, "You might as well send that thing back because I don't intend to use it." It was against my better judgment, but I called the equipment company to come and pick it up.

Up to now, due to leg weakness and shortness of breath, Bill has been able to walk only short distances by using his cane. Ever since the fall, he has been using a walker to get about the house. He sits for long periods in his recliner, and he complains of discomfort over the coccyx or tailbone area. I became concerned because he is at high risk for pressure sores due to his poor nutritional state and thin frame. I ordered a special gel foam cushion, designed to prevent pressure sores.

I also ordered a bed wedge to elevate his head at night. By now, he has returned to sleeping in our queen size bed. I always placed side rails to help him, but he was not able to turn well in the narrow bed. I kept the electric bed, which has now become the place where I lay my weary head at night. Bill still takes the BiPAP off and sleeps with the mask lying across his chest most of the night, and he has stopped using the device to exercise his lungs. I grow impatient with him at times and verbally attempt to get him to do better, and then I envision myself having to walk in his shoes.

Friday, April 23, 2004

I really was not aware of the extent of the muscle deterioration, which had occurred over Bill's body until one night recently. He came into the kitchen for a drink of water dressed only in his shorts. I was astonished at the extreme emaciation and muscle wasting over his entire body. By now, I am well aware that the disease process of ALS can cause massive muscle deterioration. I also understand that severe nutritional deficiencies, especially protein, can contribute to the muscle wasting. I think it is interesting and discouraging to realize that of all the physicians' Bill has seen (taking into account his serious nutritional problems and weight loss), not one has referred him to a dietician. Maybe some professionals assume that patients and family members have knowledge of how many food calories (in the form of carbohydrates, protein, and fat) are required in order to maintain a predetermined weight level. This would be a drastically incorrect assumption. Perhaps in our case, my being a nurse is a factor.

Since Bill will eat very little regular food, and because he has no desire or taste for the nutritional drinks by themselves, I have been searching for alternative methods to help him gain a few pounds. The most important goal is to prevent him from losing any more weight. I consulted a dietician who told me Bill needed approximately 2,000 calories a day in order to maintain his current weight of 150 pounds. She provided a recipe for a high calorie shake. I also learned about non-boiled custard from the ALS clinic nurse. This is another high calorie mixture, which is very tasty. It can be prepared in the form of custard or thinned with milk for drinking purposes. People who have kidney disease must limit protein in the diet, and they should take in only the amount of protein recommended by their physician. Since Bill does not have kidney problems that we are aware of, I add soy protein powder to the shake as well as the custard in order to provide the daily requirements for protein.

I came across an internet site that helped me to calculate what portion of the 2,000 calories should be devoted to the components of carbohydrates, protein, and fat. I have calculated that if Bill will drink at least two of the shakes each day, he will consume approximately 1,900 calories. This will be close to the calories needed to maintain his current weight, and it will provide the nutritional requirements recommended. I hope I will be able to convince him of the importance of his need for nourishment and coax him into drinking the shakes consistently. It will all depend on whether his digestive system will be able to tolerate the increase in dairy products At least I have a plan— we will see how it goes.

HIGH CALORIE SHAKE

1 can of nutritional supplement (any flavor)

1 cup ice cream (any flavor)

1 (8oz) carton egg substitute (no raw eggs)

1 tbsp sugar

Add as desired:

Any fresh or frozen fruit (strawberries, peaches, banana, etc.), chocolate syrup, or honey, Cookies…(Oreo, chocolate chip, graham cracker, vanilla wafers, etc.) Place all ingredients in a blender and blend until smooth.

NON-BOILED CUSTARD

6 cups of whole milk

1 large box instant vanilla pudding

1 (16 oz) carton egg substitute (no raw eggs)

(1/2) one-half cup of sugar

1 pint of whipping cream

2 tsp vanilla flavoring

Blend pudding and milk with a wire whisk until smooth. Blend in egg substitute. In a separate bowl, combine sugar, cream, and flavoring (beat with electric mixer for three minutes). Add this mixture to the pudding mixture and blend well. Place in a covered container and keep refrigerated.

* For thinner drinking consistency, add more milk.

The eternal God is your refuge,
And underneath are the
everlasting arms....

Deuteronomy 33:27

Twenty-two

The Everlasting Arms
Tuesday, May 4, 2004

It is springtime and the grass is growing, and Bill is anxious about the lawn care. He sat in the garage today while the yardman he recently hired mowed and trimmed the yard. Later, I overheard Bill talking to the man and arranging for him to continue to take care of the lawn. He told him about his illness and said, "I'll probably not be here next summer, and she will need a lot of help taking care of all that needs to be done around the yard." He is also worrying about washing the car, changing the air filters on the heat pump, cleaning out the garage, and numerous other activities he is unable to do. He is very frustrated. We decided to drive the car through an automatic car wash, and I vacuumed the inside. Upon returning home, he showed me how to change the air filters in the house, and he sat and watched as I cleaned out the garage. I followed his directions with sadness and sometimes tears, while discarding the items he would never use again.

I am thankful for Bill's friends who are helping by providing a few hours of diversion from his dreary existence. Last week, Jim Woody and Buster took him out to dinner, and one night he went to a movie with John Holland. A few weeks ago, we took him to see The Passion of the Christ, a movie he had expressed a desire to see. He will usually say he does not feel like going anywhere, but he will proceed to wear himself out in the process of getting ready. After each outing, he seems depressed. Following one occasion, I questioned him as to why he seemed so gloomy and he said, "Maybe it's because my friends are healthy and I'm not." One night when he came home after being out with friends, he brought me a stuffed bear. It was holding a wooden sign inscribed with the words, "You are a Special Angel." He told me it was my Mother's Day gift. I did not know it at the time, but this would be the last gift he would ever give me.

We joined the Baptist church we have been attending, but have not felt like going to church lately. One of the deacons and the senior adult pastor called and came by for a visit. They placed our name on the shut-in meal program list and said the church will deliver a meal every Wednesday, and we will receive a video of each Sunday's service. I am very thankful for a caring church family. I am also thankful that Bill's weight is currently stable due to the high calories shakes. He still eats very little solid food, and will not eat the food delivered by the church. Most of the time, he refuses to try. We are in frequent conflict over the BiPAP machine. He insists it is not working right. I am sure there is nothing wrong with the machine, and the controls are still set as the doctor ordered. Knowing that the problem lies with his lungs and not with the BiPAP, I appease him for awhile by slightly adjusting the controls. Last night, in a weak but somber tone of voice he told me, "I won't be around much longer." I believe there is a great deal of truth in what he says.

Tuesday, May 11, 2004

This is a chemotherapy day, and I am writing in the journal while receiving my treatment. I am tired because I carried a case of the nutritional supplement from downstairs to the cancer treatment room. I have been able to purchase the supplements at a lower cost, which has been a great help. Our insurance does not provide coverage unless it is given as a tube feeding and is the only source of nourishment. The fatigue I am experiencing with my many exertion causing activities is worrisome. Recently, I have noticed that after each cancer treatment, I become overly tired, weak, and short of breath just walking the short distance back to my car. I have also noticed some swelling or edema of my feet and ankles. I told the oncology nurse about these symptoms, but she did not seem overly concerned.

Kathleen and Manuel came from Saint Augustine the last of April for a visit. I was apprehensive because they had not seen Bill since the ALS has taken its toll on his body. I knew they would be shocked and upset at his appearance. We usually plan to go a few places while they are here, but this time the activities will be limited. I had previously arranged an overnight trip to a nearby inn, hoping Bill would feel like going. We took the one-hour trip to the inn on a Friday. It is an elegant facility located in a beautiful country setting and surrounded by flower gardens. That first day, Bill enjoyed the scenery, and he ate a little better than usual. He was not able to sit outside because the pollen from the flowers made his breathing worse. The overnight stay was miserable. It rained, the roof leaked on the bed, and the room was cold and damp. Throughout the night, he had breathing problems and high anxiety, and again he thought the BiPAP was malfunctioning. We were up most of the long, miserable night. Since returning home on Saturday, he has complained of constant abdominal discomfort.

The following Wednesday, Kathleen and Manuel returned home, and goodbyes were sad and tearful. They hugged Bill and told him they loved him, knowing this might be the last time they would see him. Afterwards, Bill seemed even more depressed, and the stomach problems continued. I felt the nutritional supplements were probably the cause of his discomfort. I tried holding his medication for a couple of days, but it did not help. For the past week, he has not been able to drink enough of the supplements to meet the goal of 2,000 calories, and he has lost several more pounds. One day he told me, "I'm getting worse, and I will probably be bedridden before long—maybe I'll just go ahead and die." I try not to say words that will give him false hope, so I just told him I am working hard to keep that from happening.

Monday, May 17, 2004

Bill is not talking much today because he is upset with me. It all began when I insisted he not drive anymore. He is too weak to be behind the wheel, and it is not safe for him or others. Later in the morning, he contacted the yardman that he previously hired. The shrubbery needed trimming, and he wanted mulch placed around the plants. He has been fretting about this for weeks, and his anxiety is finally relieved. He sat at the open garage door and watched to make sure the work was completed to his satisfaction. As he sat outside on his walker, I noticed that his weak attempts to stand are becoming more difficult. Until recently, he has been using a simple walker to take the solitary step leading from the den to the kitchen. Lately, he can barely lift the walker up and over the step. I found a ramp online, which fits in the doorway and allows him to use a rolling walker. The walker has a seat to allow rest if necessary. However, we had to pay for it because our insurance only pays for one walker per person. He is now too weak to manage the shower by himself, and he requires almost complete assistance with dressing. A padded bath chair with an attached stool that extends outside the bathtub, allows me to bathe him using a hand held shower. He sits on the stool, swings his feet over the tub, and slides onto the chair. Even with this small amount of exertion, bathing is an exhausting process. The shower is so hard on him, we decided twice a week would be sufficient. During difficult times such as this, he will say, "I wish it was over."

Lately, for some unknown reason, around six or seven o'clock in the evening, Bill has an episode of severe shortness of breath, which causes extreme anxiety. If he will manage to keep the BiPAP on, the breathing difficulty will be relieved back to its usual level. Preparing for sleep has become a very trying ordeal. The difficult breathing worsens the minute he lies down, and it takes about an hour for the sleeping medication to take effect. I usually sit beside the bed in order to hold the BiPAP mask in place until he finally goes to sleep. The BiPAP machine has been replaced a number of times because Bill was convinced they were defective in some way. A more recent change occurred during a storm when lightening affected the power outlet. It caused the computerized parts to malfunction. This made me realize that if the electricity should go off, the BiPAP would have no power. The home equipment company did not address this fact. I panicked, and at my request, they delivered a portable battery that provides up to three hours of power in case of an emergency.

As I write in my journal tonight, I am listening to Golden Oldies on the radio. The songs were popular in the 1950's, and they bring back a flood of happy memories. Bill and I met on a blind date when I was attending nursing school in 1956. In order to pay my tuition, I had joined the Army Nurse Corp, and I was obligated to serve two years. My first assignment was the Brooke Army base in San Antonio. We were married, Bill went with me to Texas, and we lived in an apartment just off the base. Following my discharge from the Army, we returned home. I went to work at the hospital where I trained, and Bill became a firefighter. We had our two boys, built our new home, and set about living our lives. If only we could go back from this present sorrow, and relive those days that were so full of hope and happiness. Instead, we find ourselves with one of us waiting to die, and the other facing a very uncertain future.

Tuesday, May 25, 2004

Today, I made plans to begin radiation therapy. I am thankful for anything that will keep the cancer from reoccurring again—that might save my life. I spoke with one woman in the treatment room today who had breast cancer eleven years ago. She is beginning radiation treatments because the cancer has come back in her spine. In the midst of the sadness and fear, I still find comfort in the lines of an old poem.

The Everlasting Arms

Are you sunk in depth of sorrow
Where no arms can reach so low;
There is one whose arms almighty
Reach beyond the deepest woe
God the eternal is thy refuge,
Let Him still thy wild alarms;
Underneath thy deepest sorrow
Are the Everlasting arms.

Arms of Jesus, hold me close
To thy strong and loving breast,
Til my spirit on Thy bosom
Finds its Everlasting rest;
And when time's last sands are sinking,
Shield my heart from all alarms,
Softly whispering, "Underneath thee
Are the Everlasting arms."

A. B. Simpson (1844-1919)

As for God, His way is perfect;
The word of the Lord
is proven;
He is a shield to all who
trust in Him.

Psalms 18:30

Twenty-three

What God Allows
Tuesday, June 1, 2004

The expression on Bill's face is often one of sadness and torment, and he increasingly talks about dying. I have encouraged him many times to talk about his feelings, especially about his concerns and fears. I realize it is often difficult to discuss sensitive issues, life and death issues, with those who are closest to you. While we are talking about certain heart rendering topics, he usually gets very emotional, begins to cry, and his breathing becomes more labored. The rapid breathing and tear-drenched eyes let me know that he cannot continue with the discussion. I regret I did not address these subjects with him months ago. I am thankful that John Holland comes by often, and I hope Bill talks with him about his feelings and fears. When he says, "I will die of breathing problems," considering the increasing chest muscle weakness and the smothering episodes, I fear he is right. The episodes are becoming more intense, and it occurred to me that he might need supplemental oxygen. The individual from the home equipment company tested his blood oxygen level, and it was 94 percent, which is an acceptable level. He said our insurance does not provide coverage for home oxygen unless the blood level falls below 89 percent. It would be better if health care agencies would take care of a patient's need rather than a criterion.

Amazingly, Bill can still swallow fairly well using the swallowing techniques he has learned. For the past few days, he has actually enjoyed breakfast. He has eaten a little of either cream of wheat, waffles, gravy with biscuits, or poached egg on toast. He usually drinks a high calorie shake for lunch, but very little for the evening meal. He continues to fall short on calories. The GI symptoms return almost every afternoon with indigestion, gas, and bloating. He takes medication for reflux, and we have tried numerous over-the-counter remedies, but nothing helps. I have learned that reflux and indigestion can worsen in ALS patients. As a normal occurrence, stomach acids do not flow back into the esophagus because of the strong muscles of the diaphragm. The nerve destroying process in ALS causes the diaphragm muscle to weaken, and the risk of acid reflux increases.[1] I continue to believe that the dietary supplements, as well as the clinical trial medication, are partially to blame for his abdominal discomfort.

Thursday, June 3, 2004

Yesterday, we traveled back to the ALS clinic for Bill's last appointment. The trip was difficult, and I was concerned that he might not be able to make it. He had to use the BiPAP most of the time, and I was anxiously hoping we would not have problems with the machine. We took the pre-charged battery along, but the primary source of power for the BiPAP was the cigarette lighter outlet. Restroom breaks were frequent, and managing to get him in and out of these facilities along the way was a major undertaking. Although he did not complain, he admitted to back discomfort upon questioning. It was obvious the weakened neck muscles made it difficult for him to hold his head erect. I tried to make him comfortable, but the trip was very hard on him. He was extremely fatigued when we returned home. The final muscle strength test showed continued muscle deterioration, but the FVC (breathing test) had increased from 36 percent in April to 49 percent. The increased use of the BiPAP machine was determined to be the reason for the improvement in test numbers.

I am pleased that Bill was able to complete the clinical trial, but I am glad it is over. He can stop taking the medication, and maybe the GI symptoms will improve. The ALS clinic doctor told Bill that he was not eligible for any planned clinical trials because of his diminished lung capacity. He told Bill that the need for a feeding tube was urgent, but Bill responded with, "I'll wait a while longer." Before we left, the nurse provided the name of a man in our area whose wife had recently died from ALS. He donated her wheelchair to the clinic and thought a local ALS patient might be able use it. It would be readily available, and we could avoid the cost of an expensive chair.

As Bill's hands have continued to weaken, I ordered several products that I found on the internet to assist in activities of daily living. Scooper plates have side rims that allow for pushing food onto eating utensils rather than off the plate. Non-spill cups with thick handles allow the person to drink with or without a straw. Cylindrical foam buildups tubes, when cut to size, can be placed over eating utensils, pencils, pens, and other items to allow for better griping.

Other helpful products are button guides, zipper pulls, key turners for gripping car keys, and doorknob grippers. There are multiple resources on the internet related to handicap equipment. Online links to these resources can be accessed by entering "Handicap Equipment" into the search engine on the computer. These items provide a small measure of independence, but by now, the disease has destroyed many muscle supplying nerve cells in Bill's body. He is unable to walk unassisted, his speech is less audible, he has excess saliva, breathing requires BiPAP assistance, and he is unable to eat enough to maintain adequate nutrition. He cannot bathe or dress himself, and even turning over in bed is difficult. I recall reading that the median survival rate for someone Bill's age is 17 to 18 months. This is Bill's seventeenth month. I thought about the man on the personal web site who had died when his functional rating score reached seven. An icy fear gripped my heart when I realized Bill's rating score has dropped to a current fifteen points.

Saturday, June 5, 2004

Our son, John, took me to pick up the donated wheelchair this week. It was a nice chair, but not the power chair I had expected. I thought Bill could use it temporarily, but I put the plans in motion to obtain a power wheelchair for him. The woman to whom the chair belonged was forty-five years old when she died. She had lived with ALS for seven years. Her two teenage sons were young when she received the diagnosis. Her husband told me she was never on a ventilator. I would like to have known how they coped with certain situations, what comfort measures worked best, and especially what her final days were like. However, I did not approach her husband with my questions. Since his wife's death was so recent, I felt he might not be ready or willing to share details of her illness with me. Before I left the home, we agreed that I would return the chair to the ALS clinic when Bill can no longer use it. On returning home, Bill seemed only mildly interested in learning to operate the chair. Since it was a manual one, he determined that his hands are too weak to turn the wheels. I could understand his reasoning.

I recently came across a company on the internet that makes unique vehicle seats for handicap people. In their catalog, I found a system, which I felt we needed to explore. The electrically powered seat replaces the right front passenger seat of the minivan. Using a remote control, the swivel seat turns on its base to the right. The special seat then slides along a rail from the vehicle and is lowered onto a comfortable transport wheelchair base. There is essentially no lifting for the caregiver. The wheelchair provides a method to transport the patient to wherever they need to go. The process requires an operation reversal in order to position the person back into the van. There are several adaptations for this very impressive system, and its installation is compatible to several select vehicles. The system seems to be the ideal solution for Bill's transport needs. It would be easier on him and less lifting for me. Our minivan's make and model is compatible with the mechanics of the seat, and a local company will be able to install it. One local company that does the conversion provided a quote of $9,000. This is much less than the $17,000 required for lowering the van floor and installing a wheelchair lift.

After I explained the seat to Bill, he agreed it was the best thing to do. However, he cautioned me to make certain that I took care of all the details, and he reminded me to be sure and save the original seat. It should be placed back in the van when he no longer has a need for it. In the meantime, Bill continues to use every opportunity to prepare me for his absence. One day, he asked me to take the minivan to the garage to have it serviced. I was apprehensive because this is something he has always done. He was pleased that I took care of everything as he had instructed.

Tuesday, June 8, 2004

My last chemo treatment was today, and I had my first radiation treatment. I must come to the cancer center once a week for a year to receive the antibody drug. In the meantime, I must deal with the toxic effects of the chemo. It has caused painful tingling and numbness of my fingers and toes. The nails of my fingers and toes are loose, discolored, and separating from the nail beds. I suppose this is a small price to pay in order to rid my body of the cancer. The radiation treatments will be five days a week for six weeks. The major side effect of the radiation is more weakness, fatigue, and skin problems in the area to be treated. My hair is just beginning to grow back, and like the first hair loss, the fuzz I see on my head is scarce and gray in color. It will probably grow back thin and frizzy. Somehow, the problems I have with my hair seem frivolous and unimportant.

During my cancer treatments, Bill will be home by himself approximately two hours each day. At first, I was concerned about leaving him alone, but he has done well so far. He is still able to use the phone and has the phone numbers of our nearest neighbors close by. They know when he is alone and will check on him if needed. His worsening condition tells me there is no escape from this affliction that has taken over our lives; that will eventually take Bill's life. I no longer pray for healing or remission from the disease. I only pray that he will die from a quicker and kinder cause. I pray that he will not have to experience the total paralysis, which has been his greatest fear. Most of all, I pray that God will help us to accept whatever He allows to take place in the days and weeks to come.

The patients and family members who gather in the cancer treatment room act as a support group of sorts. They feel comfortable sharing the story of their illness, their hopes and fears, with others who are experiencing similar trials. Several people know about my cancer, and they have learned about Bill's sickness. As I look around the treatment room, some are napping, some reading, and others are just waiting for treatment to be completed. It is obvious by their physical appearance which ones are farther along in their illness. Those sitting in recliners have a needle in one arm attached to bag of drug infusion; including me. I am a cancer patient, and I don't like to be on this side of the medical care spectrum. Seeing these sick people in this sad place, leaves me to wonder why God saves us from many disasters, yet allows others to ravage our mind and body. Will I ever be able to fully understand the reasons behind the suffering that God does allow?

"Though He causes grief, yet He will show compassion according to the multitude of His mercies. For He does not afflict willingly, nor grieve the children of men," (Lamentations 3:32-33)

Sunday, June 13, 2004

The radiation treatments and the lingering effects of the chemo continue to have an adverse effect on my body and mind. My red blood cell count is lower than normal, and I am physically and mentally exhausted. We are both sleep deprived and irritable much of the time. I find that I lose my patience with Bill, especially at night. After he has taken his sleeping medication, I attempt to make him comfortable in the bed. Most of the time, he is unable to go to sleep. He removes the BiPAP mask, gets out of bed, and roams around the house on his walker in the dark. He goes back and forth from the bed, the recliner in the den, the bathroom, and the living room. I must get up and stay close by—afraid he will fall. At times, I think I cannot face another trying night; but then I give thanks for each new morning and for the strength to go on.

Just in my lifetime, the cause and cure for many diseases have been discovered, but some of the most terrifying remain cloaked in secret. My greatest hope is that God, according to His infinite wisdom, will someday reveal the scientific mystery surrounding this terrible, deadly disease.

God's Will Be Done

"His will be done,"
We say with sighs and trembling,
Expecting trial, bitter loss, and tears.
And then, how does He answer us?
With blessings,
And sweet rebuking of our faithless fears.

God's Will is peace and plenty
And the power to be,
To have the best that He can give:
A mind to serve Him, a heart to love,
A faith to die, and the strength to live.
It means us all for good.

All grace, all glory;
His kingdom come and on earth begun,
Why should we fear to say,
"His will, His righteous,
His tender, loving, joyous
Will be done!"

Annie Johnson Flint (1886-1932)

But those who wait upon the Lord
shall renew their strength;
They shall mount up with wings
like eagles,
They shall run and not be weary,
They shall walk and not faint.

Isaiah 40:31

Twenty-four

A Caregiver's Anguish
Friday, June 18, 2004

Last week, the neurologist told Bill he must have a feeding tube before his breathing worsens. The doctor took great care in expressing an urgency regarding his nutritional state, but Bill continues to say, "It's not yet time for a feeding tube." He forgets that this disease has no mercy; that it allows little time for planning and reflection. It relentlessly drags the person along its course, reaping destruction on body and soul. Later, when I told him that I could not bear to watch him starve to death, he finally agreed to the feeding tube. We were able to get an appointment to see a gastroenterologist later in the week, and he scheduled the feeding tube procedure for the first week in July. Bill is to have a local anesthetic because his lung condition makes general anesthesia too risky. He will have to remain in the hospital at least overnight. I dread everything he is facing, but I am glad he will be able to receive adequate nutrition. Bill is understandably anxious about the procedure, and I can hardly bear to look at his downcast, sad expression. He must be feeling so helpless—so defeated.

For over a year, our life has revolved around doctor appointments.

Currently, all of our appointments must coordinate with my two o'clock radiation treatments. This morning, I took Bill to the ear specialist to have his hearing aids adjusted. Most of the doctors' offices are convenient, but the ear specialist's office is located in a busy uptown area where parking is a problem. Managing to get him to and from any doctor's office is becoming more of a challenge. With help, he is able to maneuver between the wheelchair and the car. This requires great effort on his part, and it is a difficult undertaking for me. Anywhere he goes, because of bouts of diarrhea, he must make frequent trips to the restroom. He always objects, but I go into the men's restroom with him. He is so weak and unsteady; he would never make it on his own. Before each doctor visit, I call ahead to remind the office staff that Bill cannot wait to be seen because he can only be off the BiPAP for a short while. So far, everyone has been very helpful and cooperative. He dreads to go to the doctor because other people in the waiting room notice how sick he is, and they will ask questions or stare. These looks of curiosity make him very uncomfortable. To add to everything else we must contend with, I am experiencing a painful, burning sensation in the radiation treatment area on my chest.

Wednesday, June 23, 2004

I lie at night and listen to the gentle cycling of the BiPAP machine. I can tell by its even, regular sound when Bill is sleeping. He groans softly each time the machine cycles to lower the pressure for exhalation, and I can hear each breath. The particular sound of the BiPAP lets me know if he removes his mask, and I get up to replace it.

He sleeps on three pillows now, having done away with the bed wedge. The wedge worked for a while to elevate his head, but as the weakness progressed, he kept sliding off. We both sleep for short periods at a time. He gets up all during the night to go to the bathroom or to his recliner in the den. Each time he changes locations, I must move the BiPAP machine and the other articles that he needs. During the daytime, I watch helplessly as he goes from one room to another attempting to find comfort. Any position, which increases the pressure on his abdomen, increases the shortness of breath. He cannot sit outside because the humidity makes breathing worse. He walks with a slow, wavering gait, with his back severely bent over. Anxious and afraid he will fall, I often remind him not to get up alone. Since his voice is so weak, I gave him his old cowbell to alert me when he needs something or wants to get up to walk. He used the bell in high school to make noise during football games. I am confident that the old brass noisemaker reminds him of much happier times.

Bill's back pain has gotten worse. On Monday, I took him to the hospital for a back x-ray. The doctor thought a slipped disc might be causing the pain. Thankfully, this was not the case. He is taking pain medication and a different medication for the GI symptoms. If he does not drink the supplements, the abdominal discomfort improves. I worry that he will not be able to tolerate the tube feeding formula. Yesterday, he told me that I needed to place him in a nursing home. He said his care is getting to be too much for me to handle. He cries occasionally, and sometimes we cry together. Each time he mentions the nursing home, I assure him that I am more than able to care for him. I will do so, God willing, as long as he needs me.

Sunday, June 27, 2004

Nothing can frighten a caregiver more than the realization of having to deal with a disease such as ALS. It is a fear that jars a person awake at night and occupies thoughts in the daylight hours. Caregivers often lose their own identity as they take on roles that are daunting and all consuming. They live with apprehension and fear of how they will be able to handle it all. Caregivers face a multitude of changes. By necessity, they must learn nursing skills and other things they have never done. They often experience the same emotional responses, including anger and depression, as the person for whom they are caring. They experience the consequences of care giving that include anxiety, worry, stress, loneliness, fatigue, intense sadness, hopelessness, and the fear of dying before the patient. Sometimes, they feel guilt because they did not do enough, were not strong enough, and did not have enough tolerance—enough patience.

Being a nurse, I have been a caregiver most of my life, but the responsibility was always shared. During my work life, I have taught care-giving skills, directed caregivers to the available resources, and served as a resource contact to many who were facing the awesome responsibility of caring for an ill or debilitated loved one. I have witnessed the initial hesitation, fear, and feelings of inadequacy experienced by those who prepare to undertake the ominous task. It was especially daunting if the patient was severely incapacitated and the care would extend over a lengthy period. Some expressed anxiety and reluctance, and I would sometimes hear comments such as,

"Maybe a nursing home would be better." However, most were more than willing to try. Many who struggled with the care giving process verbalized feelings of being overwhelmed and alone. I learned that caregivers adjust and function more effectively when they have the necessary resources and someone they can call for questions. Most of all, they need to know that they are not alone.

The emotional impact seems to be the most common bond among family caregivers. Frustration and stress are paramount because of the overwhelming responsibilities. These care-giving responsibilities are many times intimidating and complex and it is difficult to know where to turn for help and support. Normal life as it once was no longer exists due to the changing roles in family dynamics, and caregivers often become isolated from living outside the norm. They frequently feel misunderstood by non-caregivers or other family members as they struggle to do the best they can. Bouts of depression are a common factor, which can result due to the many losses, especially the loss of personal identity and feelings of isolation and hopelessness.

Over the years in my association with many caregivers, I have recognized the mounting frustration, stress, and emotional toil brought on by passing time, increasing burdens, and weariness. I have also recognized enormous strength, determination, and unfailing courage. Consequently, when my own care-giving journey began, I believed that I fully had a grasp on what it means to be a devoted and effective caregiver. I soon learned my understanding was grossly inadequate, for I had not yet walked in those shoes. In the past, during my nursing career, women were the ones who stepped forward when someone needed care. Today, care giving no longer belongs only to women.

Men make up a large percentage of the care giving population. Caring for Bill has caused me to have a deeper respect and understanding of the burdens and anguish of primary caregivers, especially those who have endured for many months or years. There must be a special place in God's heart for caregivers such as these.

When I get time, I like to read personal stories of ALS patients or their family members. Most of what I read is heart breaking and the struggles and difficulties are hard to imagine. Recently, I came across a poem written by a male caregiver in memory of his wife who had died of ALS. The poem entitled, "The Long Goodbye" demonstrates the patience, compassion, hope, and spiritual strength that are required in caring for someone who has been afflicted with this dreadful disease. It wholly captures the wounds of grief, the sadness, despair, helplessness, and hopelessness that the caregiver experiences as they watch the slow, devastating effects that this illness has on a loved one's body, mind, and spirit. The words of this heart wrenching poem touched me deeply. Every line holds true.

The Long Goodbye

(A Poem to Lorna…in Memory)

Goodbyes are not the best of times
They steal from us in petty crimes,
Like little deaths that stop the heart,
Or swiftly tear our souls apart.

Though they seem such hidden things,
They pass and often give us wings
Of faith and hope on which we fly…
Reunions after each goodbye.

We spend brief moments in farewell,
A word or two, a wish you well,
A kiss, a backward glance, a wave,
Short, poignant partings not to save.

But now, in maddening, mutant change,
Goodbye malingers in a strange
Slow motion dance of questioned pace
Where pure exhaustion ends each race.

With pain, I watch you and perceive
How imperceptibly you leave
Your ebbing strength, and shortened reach,
Your slowing walk and slurring speech,

Your frequents naps and fragile form
Your shawls and wraps to keep you warm,
Your labored breathing, quiet sighs,
The slight confusion in your eyes.

Yet knowing what must be must be,
It's time for you to lean on me.
Together, we shall walk this path
And do our best to quell our wrath.

And though the journey's sad and slow,
We'll weather it because we know
The path has surely been well trod
And leads eventually to God.

We'll pray for those who've gone before
And hope there won't be many more
The quest continues while we grieve;
The cure will come, we must believe.

We'll face our fate and trust the Lord
For courage is its own reward.
We'll count the good days one by one,
Our long goodbye has just begun.

Written in 1995 by Glen Ethier in memory of his wife, Lorna. Compiled by David Feigenbaum and published in "Journeys with ALS...Personal tales of Courage and Coping with Lou Gehrig's Disease." 1998, DLRC Press. Used by permission of the author.

Bill at a country inn
May, 2004

For He Himself has said, "I will never leave you nor forsake you." So we may boldly say:
The Lord is my helper;
I will not fear....

Hebrews 13:5

Twenty-five

Deepening Distress
Tuesday, July 1, 2004

Bill will tell anyone without hesitation that he is a "Yellow Dog Democrat." I understand the term originated in the Abraham Lincoln era when southern voters would allegedly vote for a yellow dog before they would vote for any Republican. Before Bill became ill, he was active in many fire department activities as well as in local and regional Democratic politics. He would work tirelessly for the Democratic Party during every election. In any dialogue about politics, it became clear very quickly that Bill was passionate about the Democratic Party, and he would often become fired up in any political discussion. He has met Vice President Al Gore and had a photo taken with him on one occasion, and he received an invitation to President Bill Clinton's inauguration. One day recently, a friend called to say that Bill was to receive a commendation for public service. It was to be a surprise, but I felt I had to prepare Bill beforehand to prevent him from becoming too emotionally upset. Several men from the state government came by the house this morning to present the commendation. The speaker of the State Senate, the speaker of the State House of Representatives, and the Governor of Tennessee had signed the commendation. The men did not stay long because Bill became somewhat emotional, and his breathing worsened. He seemed to be proud of the honor and took pleasure in showing it to friends and family who come by to visit.

The care giving events of last week were trying. On Friday, Bill took a different medication for his GI problems. The medication caused extreme restless legs, and he had to walk about the house find some relief. The increased activity caused more labored breathing. That night, he took a different sleeping pill, but it had an opposite effect. We were up most of the night. All day Saturday and Sunday, he was restless, short of breath, and anxious. On Monday, Bill wanted to try the new sleeping pill again, but it did not help. Most nights, we have been up until around 4:00 A.M. These long, sleepless nights leave us exhausted, short tempered, and lacking in patience. In spite of not eating, Bill continues with indigestion, bloating, and nausea. A few times, I gave him medication for nausea, which helped me when I was taking chemotherapy, and it provided some relief. He appears to be thoroughly convinced that the stomach problems are caused by this breathing machine," but he cannot breathe without it. If he takes it off, he must soon replace it. He has so many problems, and I am thoroughly exhausted. I am perplexed as to what else I can do to help relieve his discomfort.

I am sitting here tonight looking over the appointment calendar. In June, we made thirty-one trips. These included a doctor visit, a treatment or test, or some other medical related appointment, and we are not looking forward to the hospital tomorrow. Bill already has so much to deal with, and he now must face having the feeding tube procedure. He has agreed to the feeding tube, but he can still refuse to have it done. He has not refused. Having to take nourishment by artificial means is a stark reminder that we are powerless against the onslaught of this evil disease. There is almost daily evidence that it is progressing rapidly now, and I am being forced to acknowledge and accept the overwhelming fact that Bill is going to die and leave me.

Wednesday, July 7, 2004

Bill had a PEG (percutaneous endoscopic gastrostomy) tube inserted last Friday morning. With this type of procedure, the doctor places the feeding tube directly into the stomach through the wall of the abdomen. The tube extends approximately six to eight inches outside the stomach. It provides a way for the patient to receive adequate nutrition for maintaining weight and energy. If swallowing is present and not too risky, the person can continue to eat foods that are safe and enjoyable.[1] The PEG tube generally causes no discomfort, and the use and care of it is very simple to learn. Prior to being taken away to surgery, Bill looked very weak and frail lying there on the transport cart and the frightened expression on his face was troubling. I hoped the surgery would not be painful, and that the presence of the tube in his abdomen would not increase his apprehension. He tolerated the procedure, which was done under local anesthesia, without major problems. After the surgery was completed, Bill developed a severe headache and nausea. The expected overnight hospitalization became a four-day stay, because the doctor wanted to be sure that Bill could tolerate the tube feeding formula before discharge.

The care was good, but the stay in the hospital was a nightmare. Bill continued with nausea, restlessness, shortness of breath, and headache pain. He was miserable, and it was impossible to make him completely comfortable. Bill had a device attached for measuring blood oxygen levels, the BiPAP on for breathing, and continuous IVF (intravenous fluid). The tube feeding was administered slowly and continuously by pump. I was on my feet a great deal of the time helping to manage all the tubes and his many needs. When I was not on my feet, I sat in the chair beside his bed, and my feet and ankles became very swollen. Others offered to stay with Bill to relieve me, but he had so many problems and needs, I felt it would be too difficult for a friend or family member to manage. I knew he would feel more secure if I did not leave him. While Bill was still in the hospital, we received news that a favorite cousin of his had suddenly died. He was devastated over her death, which only added to his distress.

Bill would need to use a BiPAP while in the hospital, and the anesthesiologist said we could bring his own machine. The first night his breathing became much worse. Bill, being extremely anxious, told everyone, "This machine is not working right." The hospital did not permit the home equipment company, who owned the machine, to operate inside the hospital. After much discussion, the respiratory therapist was able to set up another BiPAP using the settings on Bill's machine. By this time, he was in a severe panic. Once again, He was adamant that the new machine was not working correctly. The capable respiratory therapist had to make frequent visits for troubleshooting. She was very patient by explaining how the machine worked and what Bill could do to make it work more effectively. During the chaos, his blood oxygen level dropped into the 80 percent range, and the nurse connected oxygen and gave him pain medication. Finally, he settled down and began to breathe easier. There were several more episodes similar to this during those miserable four days. My body and mind were so weary at times I thought I could not stand erect to do another task. A crucifix hangs on the wall of each patient's room in this Catholic hospital. Somehow, seeing that cross every day helped me to endure the remainder of a very difficult hospital stay.

Most people think of hospitals as places of restoration, healing, and an occasional seemingly miraculous event. This is primarily an accurate description. However, I learned early in my profession that uncertainty lurks here. Having dealt with illness and disease for many years, I am accustomed to the tragedy, which sometimes occurs inside these walls. The experience can be heartbreaking when the sick or injured person is a family member or loved one. I remember years ago, sitting and anxiously waiting by the hospital bed of my youngest brother. Gary was 24 years old when a motorcycle accident severed an artery in his right leg. The surgeon said he did not know if the leg could be saved, but we were hopeful. I remember sitting by his side following surgery to repair the damaged artery, and I watched as his leg slowly turned dark blue in color. His lower leg finally became cold, black, and gangrenous. The pain was unbearable, and Gary begged the doctor, "If you can't save my leg—just take it off." The next day, they removed the leg above the knee, and Gary has had to deal with the difficult disability all his life. Ever since that time, I have had an immense dislike for motorcycles. You can imagine my displeasure and hurt when Bill, Jr., bought a Harley.

Friday July 9, 2004

A controversy of sorts arose over the use of the BiPAP when Bill was in the hospital. He had a Living Will, which states he does not want life-prolonging procedures in case of a terminal illness. It was obvious to everyone on Bill's health care team that he appeared to be in the final stages of a terminal illness, and the BiPAP machine seemed to be causing him extreme anxiety. I was presented with the option that we needed to consider discontinuing the machine in order to relieve his anxiety and make him more at ease. It was also felt that the BiPAP, considered as a form of life support, was not compatible with his wishes in the Living Will. I was surprised and disturbed that anyone would consider taking away the BiPAP. Bill can scarcely manage to breath with the machine. I could only imagine the panic, anguish, and discomfort if he could no longer depend on it for his next breath. The actual event, when someone would remove the mask from his face and take it away, flashed through my thoughts. My mind could not even imagine such a dreadful scene.

I reviewed the literature about the BiPAP when the ALS clinic neurologist had first recommended it. The literature describes it as a non-life-support ventilation system. A person may choose this type of assisted ventilation, even though they may not want a permanent ventilator. The neurologist had knowledge of the Living Will, but he never referred to the BiPAP as life support. I disagreed with the care team's decision and explained my belief that the BiPAP is a comfort measure; not life support. To spare Bill more stress, I asked that they not discuss the topic in his presence. When Bill's lungs become so weak that he can no longer breathe on his own, the BiPAP machine, unlike a ventilator, will no longer assist breathing. The removal of the BiPAP will occur only if he specifically requests it.

Since Bill has been home from the hospital, he has tolerated four eight-ounce cans per day of the tube feeding formula. Instructions are to increase the volume in increments up to seven cans a day, which would provide 2,000 calories. Whenever I attempt to increase the amount, he complains of bloating, so I divide it into six smaller feedings. We have no feeding pump at home, so I use a large syringe and gravity flow. I follow the feeding with two to three ounces of water to prevent the tube from becoming obstructed—an undesirable situation. A small amount of clear, carbonated beverage also helps to keep the tube open. Bill sits in a chair while I give the feeding in order to prevent gastric reflux. He can eat additional food if he desire to do so. Yesterday, he asked for cake and peaches, but most of the time, he says he is not hungry. He currently weighs 137 pounds.

I received a shock when the pharmacist said that a current month's supply of the tube feeding formula would cost approximately $341. Seven cans a day (2,000 calories) will cost about $600 a month. I knew Bill would be distressed about the cost, so I chose not to tell him. He is currently able to eat only soft or liquefied foods due to fear of choking, but insurance still does not provide coverage for the formula. According to criteria, it must be his sole source of nutrition in order to be considered for coverage under our current policies. I am thankful that I am still able to purchase the new nutritional supplement through the hospital at a reduced cost. God is still at work.

I am the resurrection and the life.
He who believes in Me,
Though he may die, he shall live.

And whoever lives and believes in Me
shall never die

John 11:25-26

Twenty-six

A Turning Point
Monday, July 12, 2004

This disease has let me know that it has no mercy concerning the discomfort and problems it can cause. Recently, we have noticed that Bill's feet and legs are swelling, and his toes have shades of purple or a bluish color. The feet are so swollen he can only wear a large pair of house shoes. I had not really thought about it in regards to his illness, but it makes sense that the swelling is due to inactivity and weakened leg muscles. In a general sense, the muscle contractions used in walking helps the blood and fluid from the feet and legs flow back to the heart. When this muscle power is lost due to the effects of ALS, blood pools in the feet and lower legs. The increased pressure causes fluid to seep into the surrounding tissue. This leads to swelling or edema. The problem gets worse if the person is unable to walk about or sits most of the time.[1] Part of the swelling could be relieved if Bill were able to walk more, but walking causes extreme fatigue and shortness of breath. I tried a pair of my elastic stockings from a prior surgery, but he said they were too uncomfortable. All that remains to do for the swelling is to elevate his feet on a stool.

Bill has finally agreed to call for help when he needs to ambulate. Even when I walk with him, I do not feel confident that I would be able to support him well enough to prevent a fall. The physical therapists at the hospital use transfer belts to ambulate the patients. I was able to obtain one of these belts from an internet website. The belt is wide and fastens with Velcro around the patient's waist. It has caregiver handles, which allows adequate support of the patient's weight while walking. At the same time, it helps to prevent back strain for the caregiver. Whenever Bill is up on his walker, I always use the transfer belt for safety. The belt can also be useful when lifting or transferring someone from a chair, wheelchair, or bed.

Since Bill has been home from the hospital, a friend or a neighbor sits with him while I go for cancer treatments. Many times, Nancy or Jim Alexander will stay with him, and sometimes Buster, John Holland, or Del will sit with him. If I must go to the grocery store or drugstore for a short while, I place all the articles he needs and the bedside commode beside his chair. I always hurry to get back home because I can never be sure he will not attempt to do something he should not do. On my inquiring if he did okay, he usually says something witty like, "I ran around the block a couple of times."

Earlier today, I left a message at the doctor's office requesting a change in Bill's sleeping medication. Surely, there is something that will allow both of us a better night's sleep. He sleeps only three to four hours at night and naps often during the day. It has become an undesirable cycle of events. Several times during the night, he will want assistance to get up. His voice is so weak; he must ring his cowbell or knock on the wall to wake me. I have noticed it is becoming more and more difficult for him to climb into our higher than normal bed, and I believe it is time for a hospital bed. I also believe it is time to hire someone to assist with Bill's care. His care needs are rapidly increasing, and his condition is becoming too unstable for me to allow friends or neighbors to continue to help. I have reviewed the long-term care insurance policy criteria, and the cost for his care should fall within benefit guidelines. Sometime this week, I have to obtain separate prescriptions from the doctor for the wheelchair, the hospital bed, a gel foam mattress for the hospital bed, and a wheelchair cushion. I hope I have thought of everything.

I have delayed to initiate Bill's Long Term Care Insurance benefits because I was hoping he would live the three to five years life expectancy, which the literature described in the beginning. The insurance has fund limits, and I did not want to use the funds prematurely. The insurance lists criteria for activities of daily living that the patient must meet in order to begin to receive payment for home care services. These include the need for assistance with bathing, dressing, and transferring. Additional criteria includes being unable to prepare meals, feed oneself for nourishment, and maintain control of bowel and bladder function. In order to qualify for long term care benefits, the person applying must be unable to perform at least two of these five activities of daily living without substantial assistance from another individual. Bill should have no problem meeting the criteria requirements. A doctor's statement of his inability to perform these functions is also required. As I write tonight, I realize that if Bill's disease continues its rapid progressive course, it is doubtful that he will be able to survive for even two years.

Friday, July 16, 2004

Yesterday, I took Bill for an evaluation to determine if he qualifies for an electrically powered wheelchair. The evaluation is an insurance requirement. The testing lasted a couple of hours, and it was an exhausting trip for him. He did meet the requirements, and the therapist submitted the order for the chair. Thankfully, the medical insurance will provide coverage for the high technical chair. One additional option allows adjustment for lowering or raising the chair when transferring to and from the bed. I requested this option ($1500), even though insurance does not cover the cost. As Bill's condition worsens, it will help me to manage to move him by myself. I watched as the therapist instructed Bill in the use of the chair. I was surprised that he was able to use his hands appropriately to operate the controls. I sometimes think ordering a wheelchair is futile, but I want Bill to continue to prepare to live and to hold on to whatever hope is remaining. When I told him it would take six to nine months before the delivery of the chair, he responded by saying, "I will be dead by then." Followed by, "Even if I am alive, I won't be able to use my hands." It all still seems like a horrible dream.

I completed the last radiation treatment today. I am glad it is over because the blistering burns on my chest are painful. The topical crème prescribed provides some benefit, but the pain is never completely relieved. For the past few weeks, my shortness of breath and ankle edema has gradually worsened, and I made an appointment to see the oncologist. Following a chest x-ray, the oncologist determined I had radiation pneumonia. He prescribed an antibiotic, and the symptoms gradually improved. I have noticed that each week after I receive the antibody drug, my symptoms worsen. I remember reading about the side effects of this particular drug, and a major side effect was congestive heart failure. I am beginning to suspect that the cause of the symptoms could well be a problem with my heart. When my breast cancer reoccurred in the midst of Bill's illness, my hopes and prayers were that I would live long enough and be able to take care of him. I am beginning to worry and wonder if my own health problems are fast becoming a stumbling block for Bill's care. In this uncertain situation, I have no other alternative but to take one day at a time, be thankful, and count my blessings. Today, I am thankful that my red blood cell count has increased, which should improve my overall strength. The cancer drug treatments will be once a week instead of daily. As far as my future with cancer is concerned, it can reoccur at any time. I will have periodic follow-up x-rays and scans to check for reoccurrence, but ultimately the future will be waiting and watching to see if the cancer shows up somewhere else in my body.

Monday, July 19, 2004

The term bulbar refers to the motor neurons (nerves) located at the top of the spinal column. Bulbar dysfunction causes weakness or paralysis of the muscles that control swallowing and talking, as well as jaw, lip, and tongue movement. If an ALS patient has bulbar involvement, the condition can result in problems with swallowing, chewing, speaking, coughing, and the ability to clear saliva from the mouth and throat. There is a decreased ability to maintain an open airway during sleep and an increased tendency to aspirate food, fluid, or saliva into the lungs. Not all ALS patients have weakening of the bulbar muscles.[2] Bill is unfortunate enough to have a wide range of muscle involvement, including bulbar dysfunction. The doctor who performed Bill's swallowing test said his prior choking episodes were likely due to spasms of the larynx. Liquids or saliva can trigger these spasms by going down the wrong tube. The muscles in the throat tighten and the vocal cords close, causing a crowing sound when breathing is attempted. For a brief time, the person feels as if they have a complete blockage of the airway and they might suffocate. A spasm such as this will usually pass on its own. One can obtain immediate relief by dropping the chin down to the chest, swallowing, breathing slowly through the nose, and getting fresh air.[3] These episodes usually pass quickly, but they can be very frightening for the patient as well as the caregiver.

Bill has stopped eating entirely. He takes only ice chips and sips of water. He is tolerating, with occasional indigestion, five cans of the formula per day. He is having a serious problem with constipation, and he is often miserable with abdominal pain, nausea, and emotional distress these symptoms present. The formula contains fiber, but I must give extra fiber and stool softeners through the tube. The constipation and fiber causes him to feel an almost constant urgency to have a bowel movement. There are frequent trips to the bathroom, but he is seldom successful. He must have an enema every two to three days. We always dread enema day because it is a huge undertaking. I must administer it while he is lying down. He is unable to hold the fluid well, and it can be a very messy situation. He does not like to use the bedside commode, but he is so weak, it is a struggle to get him to and from the bathroom on the walker. Occasionally, I have had to use a rubber glove to remove the impacted bowel contents. The literature says ALS does not directly affect a person's bowel function, but indirect dysfunction can occur. The muscle weakness, caused by the effects of ALS, takes away the ability of the bearing down abdominal muscles to assist with bowel function. I have learned that once constipation starts, it can be a bothersome and vicious cycle.

Having the feeding tube inserted appears to have destroyed whatever fighting spirit Bill had left. It has marked another turning point in this journey with ALS. Bill can no longer brush his teeth, put his hearing aids in, or perform any aspect of his personal care. The ever-increasing amount of saliva causes constant drooling. He is unable to swallow the saliva, and he cannot spit it out. The limited use of his hands makes it difficult for him to use tissue to wipe the drool away. This impossible situation causes him to become extremely agitated and frustrated. No matter what I do to help, the misery continues. His functional rating score was 26 on the first day of April. The current score of nine is a stark reminder that the disease has progressed exceedingly rapid in just the past three months. It is painfully obvious that we are losing the battle. Over the years, Bill has occasionally referred to me as "Sis." Once, when I was in the process of giving him a tube feeding, he looked up at me and in a weak, sad voice he said, "Sis, I don't want to die." I was sure that my heart could bear no more.

*And God will wipe away every tear
from their eyes;
there shall be no more death,
nor sorrow, nor crying,
There shall be no more pain, for the
former things have passed away.*

Revelations 21:4

Twenty-seven

Letting Go
Thursday, July 22, 2004

The rapid progression of this most dreaded of all diseases has caused such severe muscle deterioration; it has finally robbed Bill of the ability to use his legs. He can no longer walk and must have assistance or use a cane to stand. I must use the wheelchair to take him around the house and anywhere he needs to go. When we go to the doctor, he must wear the BiPAP on the way, and then he must sit in the car with the mask on for about fifteen minutes before he is able to go in the building. The nurse always takes him back promptly to see the doctor. His voice is so weak and garbled to the extent that it is almost incomprehensible. I do most of the talking to the doctor, or I must interpret what Bill says. I am amazed that I can still understand his soft garbled speech, and I view it as a blessing. Today, we made another one of these time consuming, difficult trips to see the gastroenterologist. The doctor said Bill was doing well as far as the PEG tube is concerned. He ordered medication to help dry the excessive saliva and something for constipation. In spite of all the sadness, there has been an occasional reason to laugh. A few times, in the process of giving the tube feeding, the feeding syringe became disconnected from the tube in his abdomen. The formula splattered in our faces, arms, and clothes. It was good to hear that familiar, although short and weak, chuckle. However, all future occurrences of tube feeding splatter have been less humorous.

During a routine appointment with the doctor who performed my breast surgery, I was reminded that a prior liver scan showed multiple gallstones. He strongly advised gallbladder surgery because of the risk of rupture or infection. I explained Bill's condition, and that I would be unable to have the surgery at present, because there are always pressing issues related to Bill's care. Currently, he has a problem with excessive saliva, and the medication prescribed to dry the saliva is effective for only a few hours. I notice he becomes restless and confused after he takes it. His mouth requires almost constant wiping. Each time he wipes, it is necessary to remove the BiPAP mask, which reduces its effectiveness to assist breathing. I recently rented a suction machine from the home equipment company. The electrically powered machine has a short suction tip attached to tubing. The suction tip removes the saliva from the mouth into a glass container. At first, Bill was reluctant to have me use the suction on him. He quickly found that the suction works well to control the drooling, and he has learned to use it on himself.

To add to his anguish, he has become very sensitive to smell. I must empty and clean his urinal each time he uses it. I have stopped cooking altogether because he says the smell of food cooking on the stove is very offensive. I usually microwave soup or a microwavable dinner for myself. I have switched to scent free laundry detergent because the scented detergent I normally use on our clothes, towels, and bed linens has now become intolerable. He even believes the BiPAP mask has a pungent odor. All I can do for the mask is to wash it and clean it with alcohol. If the disease is responsible for this reaction, it is contrary to what the literature says. ALS is not supposed to affect the senses of sight, hearing, taste, or smell.

Sunday, July 25, 2004

The home equipment company delivered the hospital bed on Friday. A couple of weeks ago they delivered a wheelchair cushion, but Bill did not like it. They brought two more cushions for him to try, but neither was satisfactory. I cautioned him that he must use a cushion to prevent the development of pressure sores, but he said the cushion was too high, and it made his breathing worse. Another cushion was is too soft. I found a cushion on the internet that inflates to different levels of softness and thickness, but it took me forever to adjust it to his desired level of comfort. He is also having problems getting comfortable in bed. Last night, he slept in the hospital bed until 2:00 A.M., but then he went back to his recliner. When he sleeps in the recliner, I sleep in snatches on the couch beside him. I must make sure he does not get up in his confusion and fall; that he keeps the BiPAP on. He seems to rest better in the recliner, but the sleep is restless and disruptive. Unable to sleep myself, I lie on the couch and listen as he groans and talks erratically in his sleep.

Bill has had a computerized communication device for a couple of months. It is a rather sophisticated keyboard-based system. The technician came to the house to instruct us on its use. I thought it was a great system, which would meet Bill's needs when he can no longer talk. However, He does not use the machine, and I understand that it is not refundable. The grandchildren play with it occasionally, but otherwise, it sits idle. It is a major waste of an expensive piece of equipment. I have encouraged him to practice, but I can recall only once when he wrote, "My name is Bill Knight" across the screen. When I finally realized that Bill was not interested in learning to use the communication device, I decided to make picture boards for him to use. I found pictures to suit my purpose from an online communication aides company. I placed the pictures on three separate cardboards and labeled them with My Feelings, My Needs, and My Wants. The feelings board included pictures depicting pain, shortness of breath, hungry, thirsty cold, hot, etc. The needs board contained pictures for mask on/off, medicine, eyeglasses, tissue, hearing aids, etc. On the want board, I placed pictures requesting to lie down, turn over, sit up, watch TV, lights on/off, etc. Bill seems pleased with the picture boards. At least, when the time comes, he will have one method he can use for communication purposes.

I have arranged to initiate Bill's long-term care insurance. A nurse assigned by the insurance company came by the house to perform an evaluation on Bill. It did not take long for her to determine that we needed help. I contacted a local Christian home health care agency that a friend had recommended. The charge is $15.75 per hour, and a representative will be by next week. It will be wonderful to have help. Bill has so many care needs, and I am physically and mentally exhausted. An inner ear problem I have causes dizziness and makes matters worse. A hymn that we often sing in church has the words, "God have mercy, Christ have mercy, God have mercy on me." Most days, I find myself chanting these words repeatedly in my head. Somehow, it lifts my spirits and gives me the strength to keep going.

Thursday, July 29, 2004

They installed the handicap seat in the minivan today. When I returned home from the garage, I wheeled Bill out to the driveway to demonstrate how the seat works. He patiently watched as I proved to him that I could actually operate the controls. He tried the wheelchair, but it was very hot and humid outside, and he was having breathing problems. After only a short while he requested to go back inside. I could tell he was distressed about the seat, still not ready to acknowledge that he would require such a manner of transport. Unknown to me at the time, he would never ride in the handicap seat. I wish he could be outside more and maybe go for a ride in the van, but dealing with the daily effects of this illness takes all the strength he can muster. In addition to the constant drooling, his face is now so thin that no BiPAP face mask we have tried works to help him breathe effectively God has promised He will not allow more than we can actually bear, so He must know Bill is able to carry the burden he has been given. I do not believe he can carry it much longer. When I see the misery he must endure, I think it must be torturous beyond words to be suspended somewhere between life and death.

Someone has said that courage is the finest of all human qualities because it guarantees all the others. Bill has needed courage in his life. It takes courage to climb very high radio towers, and it requires courage to be a firefighter. Little did he know that this courage and bravery would be tested beyond anything he could ever imagine. He has fought to resist acceptance of his limitations, but he has taken each new loss with a quiet and steady resolve. Except for the physical pain and misery related to the disease, he has grumbled and complained very little. It is human nature to be afraid of dying, and being a Christian does not make one immune to this fear. A great deal of courage is required to get past the fear and find the strength required to accept and face one's death. Every day, I pray that the Lord will provide Bill with an abundance of this God given courage.

Saturday, July 31, 2004

Grief, usually defined as a deep mental anguish, is an emotional reaction to loss. People often use the word in personal stories of ALS. The emotional behaviors of denial, fear, disbelief, anger, hopelessness, helplessness, and depression are among the many wounds of grief. During these difficult months, I have recognized these behaviors, in no set pattern, in Bill as well as in myself. For the past several weeks; however, Bill's manner and behavior indicates that he is slowly but surely withdrawing from life. He sits quietly in his recliner with his eyes closed for long periods. He seldom watches TV, or reads his Bible. He often seems to be unaware of my presence in the room. He barely responds if I talk to him about family or other subject matters. He uses the BiPAP less often and for shorter periods. If I remind him about it, he will say, "I'm using it enough." I think he does not care anymore; that he has given up. Bill's appearance is so thin and gaunt; it hurts my heart just to look at him. Since he has been ill, I try not to cry in his presence. One night, as he sat in his recliner, visions of his death consumed my thoughts, and I began to cry uncontrollably. My crying usually causes him to become emotionally upset. This time, he just looked at me briefly, laid his head back, and closed his eyes. I knew then that he had already begun to leave me.

People continue to visit regularly—our sons and their wives, the grandchildren, Bill's brothers, friends, and neighbors. Everyone has been faithful. John Holland comes often to sit and talk with Bill. He has been a true friend as well as a tremendous spiritual support. It has been a blessing just to know he cares. I believe John came back into Bill's life for a special reason; to help him find peace for his soul. If there are Devine reasons for pain and suffering, one has to be that it allows a person the time and opportunity to prepare spiritually for death. I have prayed for healing for Bill over these many months, but it becomes clearer every day that God has a different plan—a plan that I must accept without further questioning. Bill will eventually receive his healing as promised, just in a different place. He seems to be at peace, and I believe he is prepared and maybe even looking forward to being free of the misery that has consumed his life. He has told me several times in the past few days that he wants to die—that he is ready.

And I will pray the Father,
and He will send you another Helper,
that He may abide with you
forever.

John 14:16

Twenty-eight

It won't be Long
Monday, August 2, 2004

"Dear Lord, Bill is so sick, and I am so tired and weary." We have spent two sleepless nights, and nerves are frayed and temperaments raw. Bill becomes totally confused and restless about thirty minutes after he takes his sleeping medication. I put him to rest in the hospital bed because it has safety rails, but he will not stay in the bed. He constantly tries to climb out over the rails. I end up by taking him to his recliner where I can watch over him from the couch. All night, he talks irrationally, hallucinates, and takes the BiPAP mask apart piece by piece. He is not aware of what he is doing. I must tape the PEG tube securely to his abdomen to prevent him from pulling it out. The confusion persists until around noontime. I stopped the medication used to dry up the secretions, thinking it could be the cause of his irrational behavior. The sleeping medication, or the fact that he may not be getting enough oxygen to his brain, could be the reason for the confusion. I have accepted the fact that I will probably never know the cause. I do know that he would be exceedingly upset and anxious, and he would not be able to sleep at all without medication.

It is impossible to rest during the daytime due to phone calls, people coming by, and so much to do. The home health nurse at the hospital recommended that we initiate home hospice care. On learning this, Bill said he would prefer to go to a residential hospice, which is located near our home. We have heard that it is a wonderful place. I discussed this with the long-term care provider, and the person on the phone said they could not assure coverage for hospice care outside the home. They probably realize that I do not have the time or energy to pursue the issue. With Bill requesting to go to hospice, I knew he must realize I am having a difficult time coping. I attempted reassurance by telling him, "We'll have help soon and everything will be okay," but my tears are always just below the surface. I find myself crying at silly, insignificant things. I cried when the credit card arrived by mail bearing his name. He cannot even sign it and will never be able to use it again. I cry when I think about coming home and he is not here. Once, he asked me why I was crying, and when I told him he said, "I won't be here anymore, I'll be in Glory."

A nice young woman from the home assistance agency came by the house today. I arranged for a nursing assistant to begin work on Friday of this week. Beginning next week, she will be here each Tuesday and Thursday from 12:00 noon until 4:00 P.M. This will allow me to go for cancer treatment on Tuesday and run errands on Thursday. These hours will permit me to give all the tube feedings. I am sure Bill is dreading having a strange female helping him with personal activities. I did consider a male attendant, but the female assistant will help with some of the household chores if necessary. I explained Bill's illness to the agency representative. I informed her of his speech problems and other physical limitations. I showed her the picture boards, which Bill has promised to use. In the course of the conversation, she wanted to know if Bill was to be resuscitated (Cardiopulmonary Resuscitation or CPR). I told her he was to have CPR in case of a sudden occurrence such as choking. I believed this to be what he wanted. After the woman left, he asked me to explain our discussion. Being a first responder fire fighter, Bill understands CPR, but I still explained it in detail. He told me, "No! I don't want that." "Why should I want CPR when I have been praying that God will take me quickly?" I promised him I would inform the appropriate person at the nursing agency of his decision not to have emergency measures.

Tuesday, August 3, 2004

Bill, Jr., came by this afternoon and visited a long while with his dad. He attempted to talk to Bill and entertain him by showing him pictures from his laptop computer. Billy has been calling and coming by more often as Bill's condition worsens. I can tell it hurts him deeply to see his father so ill and to realize he will soon die. Earlier today, Howard also came by and stayed with Bill while I went for my cancer treatment. Later, he cried and was very emotional as he related how difficult it is to see his brother's life wasting away. The almost daily deterioration in Bill's health lets us all know that time is running out. Sometimes, a family member wants to know how long I think it will be. I just tell them, "I don't think he will be with us at Christmas." Bill has talked a lot about dying lately. He says he is not afraid to die. He is only afraid of the discomfort, humiliation, and the care burden, which will result if he lives through the usual course of the disease.. He has often told me that his greatest fear is the unbearable helpless state that results from total paralysis. Once he asked me if I thought death was painful. I said it has been my experience that much of the time people seem unaware; that they just go quietly in their sleep. The Bible often refers to death as falling asleep. I told him that I viewed the moment of death to be like stepping through a door into another room—into the presence of Christ.

It has taken me the entire length of this unimaginably hard journey to accept what God has allowed in this trial. I have finally placed it all in His hands. It is with shame and regret that I recall the times when anger consumed me, and I could not pray; when I felt the Lord had abandoned us. I should have trusted Him more. Deep down, I knew God had not abandoned us, and He understood why I was unable to pray. He understood my tears, and He did not leave me in the midst of those dark times, but caused me to remember the words of His promise, that the Holy Spirit prays for me.

Likewise the Spirit also helps in our weakness,
For we do not know what we should pray for as
we ought, but the Spirit Himself makes intercession
for us with groanings which cannot be uttered.
Now He who searches the hearts knows what the
mind of the Spirit is, because He makes intercession
for the saints according to the will of God.

Romans 8:26-27

I shudder to think how I could have managed Bill's care without my nursing training and experience. I know there are those who have managed and are managing to care for loved ones who have ALS or a similar disease. They are much braver than I, and they are always in my thoughts and prayers. The need to have a nursing plan of care, to assure Bill's best care, leads me to write the following instruction for the nursing assistant.

Bill will need help with:

1. Take him to the bathroom by wheelchair, or use bedside commode. He needs help to stand and to pull his pant up/down. He will need cleaning after a BM.
2. Help him to use the urinal and empty the urinal.
3. Putting on the BiPAP mask and turning on the machine.
4. Putting in and taking out his hearing aids.
5. Raising and lowering his recliner.
6. Help to go to bed for a nap (put left side rail up). Be sure he has his bell, tissue, water, BiPAP, etc. He must have help to turn over.
7. Adjusting ceiling fans up/down. Turning lights on/off.
8. He must have help washing his hands. He will need to be shaved, have his teeth brushed etc.
9. Throw a quilt on if he is cold.
10. Get his eyeglasses and Bible as requested.
11. Help him to move to another room or chair (use transport belt). Keep his feet elevated while sitting. Place the gel foam cushions in the chairs.
12. Answer the door and phone and take messages.

*Call Shirley's cell phone for questions, problems, or any other reason.

Wednesday, August 4, 2004

Our son, John, and his family came by to visit this afternoon. The two young grandsons kissed Bill on the cheek and said, "I love you Papaw." This brought a smile to his face, but after visiting for a short while, he said he was tired and asked to go to bed. I remember bygone days when Bill would take pleasure in teasing all the little fellows. He would try to shock them by flipping his false teeth out at them, and they always wanted to see him flip the teeth again. I had a picture of a baby monkey on the refrigerator, and he told them it was a photo of him when he was a baby. They believed him until they got old enough to know better. They are going to miss their Papaw.

Bill has slept in the den in his recliner for the past several nights, and I have attempted to rest on the couch beside him. Twice this week, he has awakened in an unusual happy mood. With a smile on his face, he told me, "Mother came to see me last night." He said he was very happy to see her, but she was sad because he did not let her know about his illness. Bill was always close to his mother—he loved her very much. Before he became ill, I saw him cry only twice. He cried when we learned I had breast cancer, and he cried when his mother died. Perhaps her visitation in the night was nothing but a dream, or maybe it was a vision sent down from Heaven.

I have always believed in angels. I believe they protect us on Earth and assist us on our way to Heaven. The Bible says, "*Are they not ministering spirits sent forth to minister for those who will inherit salvation?*" (*Hebrews 1:14*). Angels can present themselves in any form or shape that God desires. They can come disguised as another human being or in a dream as they did in Biblical times. Only the Lord would have the compassion to send comfort, just when Bill needed it most, in the image of a beloved mother. Whatever he experienced, it seems to have brought him great peace. He has told me several times since his mother's appearance, "It won't be long."

During these long, dreadful nights, when I am finally able to lay my head on my pillow, my thoughts rush ahead to the immediate future and the misery that Bill will ultimately have to endure. I yearn for sleep, but thoughts such as these do not allow this blessed escape. I lie there listening to the noise of the BiPAP machine and his labored breathing. I can tell by the sound when he is resting, or when he is having problems in the night. Each night, I close my eyes and pray that he can rest and be at ease.. Any amount of sleep for Bill is such a wonderful blessing, and I am thankful that he is able to forget, if but for a little while, this present anguish. Sometimes, the Holy Spirit puts a scripture in our heart that provides peace and comfort when we need it most—when we are very troubled or heavily burdened. When I am finally able to close my eyes, I remember this scripture. It causes me to imagine that the Lord has spread His great wings over our house, and I am comforted.

And He shall cover you with His feathers,
And under His wings you shall take refuge;....

Psalm 91:4

*Peace I leave with you, My peace
I give to you;
Not as the world gives do I give to you.
Let not your heart be troubled,
neither let it be afraid.*

John 14:27

Twenty-nine

He Himself is Our Peace
Wednesday, September 4, 2004

It was evident when August arrived that Bill's illness was quickly advancing to cause complete paralysis—the locked in state that he so dreaded. It was becoming more difficult for me to move and lift him by myself. I began to make plans in my mind to care for someone who is mostly in a bedridden condition. The fourth day of August was on a Wednesday. It was another miserable day, which followed a sleepless night of confusion and restlessness. The misery was obvious in Bill's inability to find a position of comfort, struggling to breathe, and the aggravation of having to deal with the excessive drooling. At bedtime, I gave him the sleeping medication and prepared him for bed. In his weak, raspy voice he told me he did not want to sleep in the hospital bed anymore. I helped him into our queen-sized bed, but he required more help than usual. He was unable to turn over or help by pushing himself up in the bed. This was a definite change, and I made a mental note to look into getting a patient lift.

These lifts function by using a seat in the form of a sling attached to the lift. The lift operates by lifting the patient to and from a bed or chair with less effort by the caregiver. Even with a lift, I would need help. I would have to have a home care assistant for more than four hours a day. On this night, using an old nursing maneuver, I placed a folded sheet under Bill and used it to turn him on his side. I adjusted the covers and placed all the necessary items within reach. When I bent down to kiss him on the cheek, he took my hand and kissed it. After placing the BiPAP on, I sat with him for a while, and then I went into the den where I could release my stored up emotions with a flood of tears. Even with a room between us, I could still hear his noisy groans and labored breathing. The anguish and desperation I felt are impossible to describe. "Please Lord, if healing is not possible; don't let him suffer any longer."

Bill slept unusually well that night, and he kept the BiPAP on. He awakened twice to use the urinal. Around 7:30 A.M., he said he was ready to get up, and I helped him to sit on the bedside. I put on his robe because it was a cool morning. When I helped him into the wheelchair, I noticed that the swelling had gone down in his feet and legs. I wheeled him into the den and into his recliner. I asked if he wanted the BiPAP on, and he responded, "I believe I do." His breathing seemed no worse than usual. He appeared to be resting, so I went into the bathroom. Gone less than five minutes, I came back into the room and noticed that Bill's head had dropped forward, and he was obviously not breathing. I called his name, but he was unresponsive and I could not feel a pulse. I remember crying out, "Oh, Bill—No!" I was immediately aware that the Lord had quietly stolen him away, for I had heard no sound. For an instant, the nurse in me wanted to attempt to revive him with CPR, and then I remembered his wishes. Bill went to be with the Lord at 7:45 A.M. on August 5, 2004. Later, I felt sure that God had heard my anguished cries. He caused Bill's sleep to be unusually restful during his last night on earth, and He mercifully removed me from experiencing the moment of his death.

Bill had wanted to escape the total paralysis caused by this disease. He desired to die quickly, and his prayers were answered. After the initial shock, my first thought was that Bill was alone when he died. Then I remembered the promise, "I will never leave or forsake you." Never means not at any time, and this promise is true in life as well as the time of death. Bill was not alone. I wanted to be with him when he died, but God did not deem it so. Perhaps He wanted to spare me the memory. In the midst of this terrible grief, comfort comes only with the realization that Bill, when he took his last breath, became cured of a disease that had caused him much pain and suffering. I can only imagine the joy when he left his disease-ravaged body behind and became free from all his misery.

I remember the events of the remainder of that morning as if being in a fog or mist. I remember calling our next-door neighbors, and Del and Drama came. I must have seemed in a state of shock, for Del suggested that I contact 911. When I told the dispatcher that my husband had died, she wanted to know, if someone was performing CPR. I explained that Bill had a terminal illness and that his Living Will stated no resuscitation. The emergency ambulance came, the police came, and I answered many questions. Several forms were completed, and someone requested a copy of Bill's Living Will. I called our sons, and they came quickly. Good friends Susan and Brenda came and straightened up the house. Brenda and Drama also brought food. The mortuary ambulance came, and I covered Bill up with one of his mother's quilts. When they took his body away, the pain I felt was as if my heart was tearing from my chest. Somehow, I managed to get through the rest of the day. That night, as I laid my weary head down on the same spot where he had slept only a few hours before, a profound sense of loneliness overwhelmed me, "What will I do without him?" Every moment since that day has seemed like an unreal dream. Even when death is expected, and it comes after a long, devastating illness, one is never prepared. Bill's illness and death have shaken my world unlike anything else. It is a painful reality—a reality that has left a void that is impossible to explain and can never be filled.

Family, friends, and neighbors helped me during those difficult days that followed. I barely recall making funeral arrangements. Many people came to the family visitation. My feet and ankles were very swollen, and I was so tired and weary I could barely stand during the service. The Fire Department Honor Guard kept vigil on both sides of Bill's urn, adding a special meaning and dignity. I remember that young Sean wanted to know where Papaw's body was. It is exceedingly difficult to explain cremation to a young child. John Holland gave the eulogy on the day of Bill's funeral. He told of their friendship growing up and their visits during Bill's illness. He read Bill's favorite verse of scripture, *"For God so loved the world that He gave His only begotten Son, that whoever believes in Him should not perish but have everlasting life,"* (*John 3:16*). At my request, John read a poem with the title, "He Leadeth Me." Someone gave me the poem for comfort purposes during an earlier difficult time in my life, and it has a special meaning. When the service ended and the bagpipes played their haunting version of Amazing Grace, it revived a crushing sense of grief and loss.

Kathleen and Manuel stayed with me for ten days after Bill's death. It was good not to be alone. I dreaded the time when I would have to face the empty house—the loneliness. In the process of attempting to cope with Bill's death, I learned that there is a physical pain as well as an emotional pain to grief. It is a constant, heavy ache in the chest, which cannot find relief. People often say, "Time heals all wounds," but I do not believe we get over the loss of a loved one. We just get through it for a time, and then we make an effort to go on without them. The plans and dreams we hold so dear are meaningless in the end. One life storm can come and wash them all away.

Last week, my son John went with me to choose a monument for Bill's grave. The woman at the cemetery office was kind and helpful, but I was numb mentally and having problems concentrating. Even knowing that Bill would not live, I had given little thought to a grave marker. I had no idea what would be appropriate, but I had one requirement. The monument should have a permanently attached vase, because keeping flowers on Bill's grave would be important to me. It hurt my heart to have to look through the catalog of gravestones, and I had to make myself continue. There were so many types and sizes, which made the task even more difficult. I finally settled on a double marble monument with a vase on top. I chose a type of marble called Tennessee Pink. I was relieved as we left the cemetery office to return home, and I hoped I would never have the need to choose another gravestone—it is too painful.

During the course of the following days, I searched for a meaningful verse of scripture for engraving on Bill's monument, but I was having difficulty finding the right verse. One evening, I picked up his daily devotional book and read the Bible verse in Ephesians 2:14 that he had marked to read for August 5—*"He alone is our peace."* The devotional message ended with this sentence, "Whatever wars rage in your life, lay them at the foot of the cross, and ask Jesus to give you His peace."

A pink marble stone

He Leadeth Me

Psalm 23:2

"In pastures green?" No, not always.
Sometimes He, who knoweth best,
In kindness leadeth me where heavy shadows be;
Out of the sunshine warm and soft and bright,
Out of the sunshine into the darkest night.
I oft would yield to sorrow and affright,
Only for this, I know he holds my hand;
So whether led in green or desert land,
I trust, although I may not understand.

"And by still water?" No, not always so.
Oft times the heavy tempests round me blow,
And o'er my soul the waves and billows go.
But when the storm beats loudest, and I cry
Aloud for help, the Master standeth by,
And whispers to my soul, "Lo it is I".
Above the tempest wild I hear Him say,
"Beyond the darkness lies the perfect day;
In every path of thine I lead the way."

So whether on the hilltops high and fair
I dwell, or in the sunless valleys where the
Shadows lie, what matter? He is there;
And more than this, where'er the pathway leads,
He gives to me no helpless, broken reed,
But His own hand, sufficient for my need.
So where He leads me I can safely go;
And in the blessed hereafter I shall know
Why, in His wisdom, He hath led me so.

       Author unknown

In my Father's house are many mansions:
If it were not so, I would have told you.
I go to prepare a place for you.

And if I go and prepare a place for you,
I will come again and receive you to Myself;
that where I am, there you may be also.

John 14:2-3

Thirty

Memories
Tuesday, February 15, 2005

The brilliant color of the flowers stands out against the muted pinkish gray of Bill's monument. I carefully arrange the artificial roses in the vase in spite of the bitter cold. Bill would be pleased that I chose red roses—his mother's favorite color. Bill has been gone over six months, but grief is still new. During those six months, I learned that the Lord was not finished with my testing. When Bill was struggling with his illness, I had shed enough tears to last a lifetime, but I had not cried since the night before he died. One evening after the funeral, I sat staring at his empty chair, and I was suddenly overwhelmed with grief and sadness. The space that my husband had occupied on this earth was empty. He was gone forever. Stored up emotions brought violent tears. The crying, which can only describe as a grief stricken wailing, went on for a while. With tears spent and the wailing over, I knew that I had to face reality—to try to go on. I have attempted to keep busy, trying not to dwell on the sorrow. One week, I washed the walls of every room in the house, but grief still followed me around. The most difficult task was to dispose of Bill's clothes. At first, I could hardly bear to open the closet door because just the sight of his shoes brought tears. After a few weeks, I found comfort in stroking his jacket or a favorite shirt. It took several months before I was finally able to pack up his things and give them away. Some special personal items, I keep stored away in a box. His red firefighter jacket and winter robe still hang in the hall closet.

I had ignored my unexplained symptoms at first, but during the weeks following Bill's funeral, my shortness of breath, fatigue, and feet and ankle swelling worsened. My family physician referred me to a cardiologist. When I was finally able to obtain an appointment, the doctor said my heart's pumping efficiency was dangerously low. The diagnosis was heart failure, which was attributed to a previous cancer drug. While sitting on the examination table, even before the doctor examined me on that October morning, I was already suspicious that my recent heart palpitations were probably serious in nature. The cardiologist told me that I had a dangerous heart rhythm disturbance in addition to heart failure. He made arrangements to admit me to the hospital. He recommended that I have an EP study (electrophysiology study) to better access the cause of the heart irregularity. I refused the study because I believed if the heart failure was under control, the heart rhythm problem would get better. I also told him I did not want a pacemaker or implanted defibrillator, which is the common treatment for this type of rhythm disturbance. Bill was gone, and I really did not care whether I lived or died. The doctor was kind, but he looked at me in disbelief when I asked that my hospital record be labeled with DNR (do not resuscitate), which means no treatment for heart or respiratory arrest. I suppose he understood because he did what I asked.

I did agree to go to the hospital for treatment of the heart failure, and I became a patient on the same cardiac unit where I was a nurse manager for many years. I had hired many of the nurses on the unit, and I knew most of the nursing staff. They are excellent nurses who took very good care of me, but I missed Bill. I have been in the hospital a few times over the years, and I always had him to depend on. He would stay with me if needed, and he would run errands and bring the things I needed from home. This time, he was not there, and I felt so alone. I made it through the acute stage of the illness, and my heart rhythm returned to normal. I will always have heart failure because there is no cure. It is possible to control the symptoms with medications, a low sodium diet, and heart strengthening exercise. I was still in a gloomy and depressed state when the Christmas season arrived. I dreaded facing the first Christmas season without Bill. In the past, we always celebrated with our children and their families on Christmas Eve. This year, sadness will overshadow the cheer because one will be missing. On Christmas morning, Bill and I always went to our sons' homes to see the gifts that Santa had brought for the grandchildren. I managed to go there alone on Christmas day, but it felt strange and sad. Nothing will ever be the same.

I will always remember the overwhelming sense of apprehension, despair, and fear when we first learned that Bill had ALS. The desperate search for information only served to paint a picture that was bleak, grim, and seemingly hopeless. I chose to keep most of what I learned to myself. I knew it would only add to Bill's anguish if he had complete knowledge of the trouble that lay ahead. He frequently wavered between feelings of hopefulness and hopelessness, and was often bewildered as to why he was stricken with one of the worst of all diseases. I watched in an agony of my own as he struggled to cope with the physical losses caused by the disease. Sadness and fear accompanied each loss as his illness forced him to relinquish his independence to devices, aides, and to me the caregiver. I witnessed his spiritual struggle as he sat reading his bible, hoping to find peace and discover a purpose for it all. ALS is a devious affliction, and it stole many things from Bill, but it was never able to take away his wry and indestructible sense of humor.

There is no doubt that my nursing training and experience were invaluable in caring for Bill. I could not imagine how someone with no medical background or nursing skills would be able to deal with such an enormous challenge. The gathering of a mass of information in order to educate myself about the disease proved to be the most valuable of all my endeavors. Keeping records of equipment, pertinent medical resources, helpful websites, and important phone numbers provided the necessary references when my brain could store no more. Keeping a journal became a tremendous blessing. It provided a method to record and track important events, to evaluate Bill's progress, and anticipate his needs. It helped to relieve daily stress and anxiety. I could pour out my fears, feelings, and frustrations onto its pages. In the process of writing, I could believe I had some degree of control over my shattered life. I remember reading somewhere, "When life breaks you, God can make you strong in the broken places." Before it was over, I had many broken places that needed His attention.

ALS is not only a disease of the body; it is an affliction of the heart, mind, and soul. The body receives the life-threatening blow, but each person must learn to cope with the illness in their heart and mind. Hope is always the essential guiding force for the soul. Each person handles adversity according to their own beliefs and values, and there is no correct or wrong way. Individual courage and bravery can take different pathways depending on the person and the circumstances. Some people desire to be in complete control of their situation, and they seek to learn everything there is to know about the disease or condition. They may become active in a support group and seek to do all they can to live as fully and as long as possible.

Some people might make a decision to live on a ventilator. Perhaps these are the most courageous of all. Other people, like Bill, may desire to know only the basics of their disease, and they are not comfortable sharing their feelings in a group setting. They choose to deal with the disease and its consequences on their own terms. If he had been younger, Bill probably would have agreed to treatments that were more aggressive, but he did not want to live a restricted life. He was adamant about his decision not to have a ventilator. He chose instead to let the disease take its ominous course on his body, while he prepared spiritually to die. He was finally able to say, "I am ready." For some people, dealing with a fatal diagnosis seems unthinkable, unacceptable, and unbearable. As in the Doctor Jack Kevorkian story, they may choose not to deal with the disease at all. In fact, there were times when I was fearful that Bill might ask me to assist in his early death, but he was aware of my beliefs; that I could never participate in taking a life even to relieve suffering. I prayed that any thoughts of suicide would be erased from Bill's mind, and that He would find the strength and courage to face whatever the illness required. I believe my prayers were answered because he never indicated a wish to end his own life—even in the darkest moments.

Looking back, there are things I would do differently if given a chance. I would set chores aside just to sit with Bill more. I would have enlisted help with his care much sooner. I would have more patience and understanding when he could not find the strength or the will to help manage the effects of his illness. Now, all I have is memories. I can find memories in the chili recipe written in his quaint left-handed style, the tools hanging in the garage, the room that he built, and the many keys that he kept in a metal box. I have not yet been able to determine what locks those keys fit. Many times, the tear filled memories blot out the good ones. An inscription on an old headstone says it all, "Death leaves a heartache no one can heal—Love leaves a memory no one can steal." Bill's brother, Howard, has a talent for writing poetry. He wrote this poem reflecting his memory of a little four-year-old boy helping to choose a name for his baby brother.

> When I was very young, my mother said to me,
> If you had a little brother, what would his name be?
> I don't know why I liked it, but I do to this day still,
> I said, why don't we name him…just plain Bill.
>
> They named him William Kenneth, it was ok you see.
> No matter how you say it, it's always Bill to me.
> As little brothers often are, sometimes he was a pain.
> But oh, what I would give today to have him back again.

If we are ever so bold as to doubt God's wisdom, we only need to reflect on the blessings He bestows in the form of memory. When a loved one passes away, we are left a treasure chest of memories. It is one gift that death cannot take from those who remain. However, the mind may unconsciously struggle, mentally and emotionally, to accept that a loved one is truly gone; that the space they once occupied on earth is vacant or unfilled. Sometimes, when I am by myself at home, when it is very quiet, I think I hear Bill call my name. Somewhere in the depths of my memory or imagination, I hear the particular sound of his truck pulling into the driveway, then familiar footsteps. Now and then at night, in my half-asleep state, I seem to be aware of a recognizable movement on the side of the bed as if someone has sat down. I realize these imaginings are some curious feature of deep memory or flight of awareness that is beyond my understanding, but in some way it is consoling and reassuring.

I think of Bill every day, and I am trying very hard not to dwell on his suffering. I try instead to picture him in Heaven where he is happy, well, and present with the Lord. Sometimes, when grief comes near, and its burdens become especially heavy, I put on Bill's old robe, and I wrap myself in memories.

In this dark world of sin and pain,
We only meet to part again.
But when we reach that heavenly shore,
We there shall meet to part no more.
The joy that we shall see that day,
Shall chase our present grief away.

                          Author unknown

Epilogue

August of 2010 marks the sixth anniversary of Bill's death. It marks six years that I have been cancer free. With the help of family and friends, I am still learning to adjust to managing life by myself. Even though it holds sad memories, I have managed to remain in the house where Bill died. I hold his memory close, and I miss him especially on his birthday and other special holidays. I wish he were here when I had to make decisions for the failed heat pump, a leaking water heater, and the skunk that died under the house. I miss him most of all when there are no strong arms to hold and comfort me in times of trouble and sorrow.

Whenever I search the internet for information relating to any advances in the treatment of ALS, I find that research is ongoing on several fronts. Researchers are still exploring environmental agents, toxins, inflammation, and other factors related to the development of ALS. Current research includes gene therapy and stem cell clinical trials. However, the wicked affliction continues to kill and bestow its merciless devastation on many lives. Rilutek remains the only drug available for treatment. Several months following Bill's death, I learned that he was taking the real Celebrex used in the clinical trial, but it failed to show any benefits for patients diagnosed with ALS.

Bill once told me, "I'll never live to see the grandchildren grow up." Today, when I visit his grave I tell him about the four boys and the little girl he did not live to meet. The oldest grandson, Justin, is eighteen. He graduated from high school this year. Just before graduation, he went on a trip to Europe. He loves music, enjoys playing the guitar, and composing his own songs. John Morgan turned sixteen this summer. He completed his first year of high school in a prestigious academy because of his excellent grades. He gave us a fright before Christmas when he had to undergo back surgery for a spinal tumor. Thank God, the tumor was not cancerous. Sean is now twelve-years old, and he is doing well in school. In his quiet, serious, steady way, he always strives to do what is right. He enjoys playing the drums and is a member of the school band. Ten-year-old, Andrew, who was only four when Bill died, is in the Boy Scouts. He does well in school, loves video games, and is very good at drawing. He is a caring, thoughtful boy who often surprises us with his insightful and clever statements. Bill would be pleased that the little boys he loved so much are growing up and doing well.

Emma Grace was born almost a year after Bill's death. We celebrated her fifth birthday on July 19. She is the blonde, blue-eyed little granddaughter Bill always wanted to spoil. She is a total girl who likes Barbie dolls and ballet. Emma Grace knows her papaw Bill is in Heaven, and she will ask questions about him. When she dresses up to play Princess, she refers to his high school photograph as her "Prince Charming." One day, Del, our neighbor who has gray hair, was doing some work in my yard. She was very excited when she came running to tell me that Papaw had come home from Heaven and was mowing the yard. I believe Emma Grace came to fulfill God's promise, "*I will turn their mourning into joy.*" (*Jeremiah 31:13*).

I love my children and grandchildren; they are my life. My prayer for each of them is that they receive Christ as Savior and live useful, moral lives according to Biblical principles. Before I die, it would be wonderful to have the assurance that I would see them all again someday.

Andrew, Justin, Emma Grace
John Morgan and Sean
The Knight Grandchildren July 2009

Since Bill's death, in addition to his brother, Jim, we have lost Howard's wife, Peggy, my sister, Jean, and my good friend, Betty. My niece, Millie, sustained fatal injuries from a car accident. She was only thirty-two years old. Several of Bill's firefighter friends have passed away. It seems that pain, tragedy, and sorrow are never ending. When adversity comes and peace is shattered, it is difficult for us to make sense of it all. Why we must travel through valleys of darkness is often bewildering, but God is able to help us bear the burden and navigate the darkness. He can meet us in our adversity and use it to make a difference for someone else.

This journey has taught me many valuable lessons. I have learned that strength and courage exist for our trials beyond what we believe to be humanly possible; that after the darkness passes, life still manages to go on. As to the reason for terrible tragedy, I suppose there is no reason or justification anyone could give for disaster or adversity that we would be capable of understanding. Only God knows. I only know that my human resolve and self reliance were severely tested, and I was drawn closer to God. My faith is much stronger now, and I will be better prepared for other life trails that are sure to come.

In the darkest moments of this journey, there were times when I did not have a desire or the will to pray, but God listened to my tears. By His guidance, I was able to access the information and resources needed to care for Bill. He was my counsel when there were painful and difficult decisions to make, and even though the cancer tested my resolve, there was strength for each day's tasks. Courage attended me when hopelessness thrived. I prayed for peace when I was worn and weary, and peace came. I experienced compassion when He provided comfort and support through the love and kindness of family, friends, and neighbors. He watched over us during the long, fear-filled nights, and there were many. He was my refuge when I was lost in the darkness of grief. I witnessed His mercy when the cancer treatments were effective, allowing me to live and be able to care for Bill.

I prayed for God's abiding presence, and He stayed—drawing nearer when we needed Him most. He enclosed us with His goodness and grace and provided everything needed to weather the storm. I prayed that Bill could be relieved of suffering, and the Lord's mercy abounded when his terrible trial ended on that cool August morning. Finally, I asked God for His help, for the courage and the will to tell this story, hoping it could serve to help someone else. Today, I am writing the last paragraph of the last page. God keeps His promises, and His word always points to those unchanging truths and everlasting promises. The promise of eternal life, to be with the Lord and see Bill and all my loved ones again, is the most precious promise of all.

> There is a living God;
> He has spoken in the Bible;
> He means what He has said;
> He will do all that He has promised.

James Hudson Taylor (1832-1905)

Taylor, J. Hudson. n.d. *Quotes and Notes* Accessed 11 Nov., 2010 Available from <http://www.wholesomewords.org/devotion7.html

End Notes

Chapter 3
[1] MDA, "Diseases of the Neuromuscular Junction" (National Muscular Dystrophy Association, 2010). http:/www.mda.org/diseases/mg.html.

Chapter 4
[1] ALSA, "Diagnosing ALS": Patient Services, FAQ (The ALS Association, 2009) <http://www.alsa.org/print.cfm?title=Diagnosing%20ALS&URL=als%2Fdiagnosing%2Ecf...

Chapter 5
[1] ALSA, "What do the Words Amyotrophic Lateral Sclerosis Mean?" : What's It All About, (The ALS Association Living with ALS- Maunal 1, 1997, revised 2007), 9.
[2] Ibid., "Why is ALS also referred to as "Lou Gehrig's disease?" 9.
[3] Ibid., "What type of nerves make your body work properly?" 12.
[4] Ibid., "What are motor neurons? "What do motor neurons do? 10, 11.
[5] Ibid., "What causes nerves to die?" 15.
[6] Ibid., "What is not affected by ALS? "How will ALS affect you? 26, 27.
[7] Ibid., "What are some of the signs and symptoms of ALS? 19, 20.
[8] Ibid., "What are the types of ALS (Sporadic, Familial), 22.
[9] Ibid., "When, and how likely is it for ALS to occur? 21.
[10] Ibid., "What kinds of treatments are available for ALS?", Rilutek. 21.

Chapter 7
[1] ALSA, "What are some theories about motor neuron degeneration and the development of ALS?": What's It All About, (The ALS Association Living With ALS, Manual 1, 1997, revised 2007), 17, 18.
[2] ALSA, "New research involving Gulf War veterans could provide insight about ALS," (The ALS Association, Sept. 22, 2003) <http://www.alsa.org/print.cfm?title-New%20Research%20Involving%20Gulf%20War%20...

[3] ALSA, "Forms of ALS" (The ALS Association, 2011) <http://www.alsa.org/print.cfm?title=Forms%20of%20ALS&URL=als%2Fforms%2Ecfm%3...

Chapter 10
[1] Roberta Friedman, Ph.D., "ALS and Clinical Trials" (The ALS Association, September 29, 2005) <http://www.alsa.org/print.cfm?title=ALS%20and%20Clinical%20trials&URL=patient%2...

Chapter 11
[1] ALSA, "How Can You Determine How Well Your Lungs are Functioning?": Adapting to Breathing Changes, (The ALS Association Living with ALS Manual 6, 1997, revised 2007), 21, 22.
[2] ALSA, "Northwest ALS Consortium Clinical Trial of Celebrex in People with Amyotrophic Lateral Sclerosis", (The ALS Association, Update- October 25, 2004) <http://www.alsa.org/patient/drug.cfm?id=47

Chapter 15
[1] The University of Massachusetts Medical school, Center for Outcomes Research, The ALS C-A-R-E Program (copyright 1995-2011) http://www.outcomes-umassmed.org/alsscale.aspx

Chapter 16
[1] Michael White and John Gribbin, A Life in Science, (copyright 1992, 1998, 2002, all rights reserved- The First edition by Viking, 1992), "Doctors and Doctorates", Chapter 4, 62, 63.
[2] Neal Nicol and Harry Wylie, Between the Dying and the Dead- Doctor Jack Kevorkian's Life and Battle To Legalize Euthanasia (copyright 2006, all rights reserved), "Defending Himself", Chapter 12, 218-223.

Chapter 18
[1] ALSA, "Braces (orthosis)": Functioning when Your Mobility is Affected- (The ALS Association Living with ALS Manual 4, 1997, revised 2007), 20.

Chapter 19

[1] ALSA, "Reacting to the Diagnosis- the Author's Observation": Coping with Change, (The ALS Association Living with ALS Manual 2, 1997, revised 2007), 15.

Chapter 20

[1] ALSA, "BiPAP-S/T": Adapting to Breathing Changes, (The ALS Association Living with ALS Manual 6, 1997, revised 2007), 31.
[2] Ibid., "Decreased Cough Effectiveness", 13.
[3] Ibid., "Breathing Problems During Sleep", 14.
[4] ALSA, "Adapting to Breathing Changes and the Use of Noninvasive Ventilation", Living with ALS video (The ALS Association, 1997, revised 2007)

Chapter 21

[1] ALSA, "What are Some Effective Cough Techniques (The Cough Machine)?: Adapting to Breathing Changes, (The ALS Association Living with ALS, Manual 6, 1997, revised 2007), 19,20.

Chapter 23

[1] ALSA, "Acid Indigestion": Managing Your Symptoms and Treatment, (The ALS Association Living with ALS, Manual 3, 1997, revised 2007), 21.

Chapter 25

[1] ALSA, "What if You Cannot Consume Enough Food...(PEG Feeding Tube)": Adjusting to Swallowing and Breathing Difficulties, (The ALS Association Living with ALS, Manual 5, 1997, revised 2007), 18.

Chapter 26

[1] ALSA, "Swelling of the Hands and Feet": Managing Your Symptoms and Treatment, (The ALS Association Living with ALS, Manual 3, 1997, revised 2007), 17.

[2] ALSA, "Loss of Bulbar Function and Breathing Difficulty": Adapting to Breathing Changes, (The ALS Association Living with ALS, Manual 6, 1997, revised 2007), 13.

[3] ALSA, "Laryngospasms": Managing Your Symptoms and Treatment, (The ALS Association Living with ALS, Manual 3, 1997, revised 2007), 20.

Helpful Websites

1. www.alsa.org   The ALS Association.
2. www.als-md.org   ALS division of The Muscular Dystrophy Association.
3. www.bruno.com   Bruno Independent Living Aids.
4. www.communicationaids.com   Communication Aids.
5. www.dynovoxtech.com   Communication Devices.
6. www.foodservicedirect.com   Thick-It Food/Liquid Thickener.
7. www.nfcacares.org   National Family Caregivers Association.
8. www.jhemerson,com   Cough Assist Machine.
9. www.mayoclinic.com   Health and Medical Information.
10. www.neurologychannel.com   Health and Medical Information.
11. www.posey.com   Health Care Products.
12. www.rohogroup.com   Health Care Cushions.
13. www.sheerbalance.com   Nutrition Calculators.
14. www.thewrightstuff.com   Health Care Products.
15. www.webmd.com   Health and Medical Information.
16. www.wily.com   Easy Chew- Easy Swallow Cookbook.